"This is a troubling book. It is troubling in part because it places the laser light of truth on one of the sore spots of the Christian organizations around us. It also challenges us to quit whining or adopting the convenient 'victim' attitudes that are easily at hand in our culture. The Baldas do not provide comprehensive solutions or simplistic ones. But they do make a valuable contribution to the conversations and the work that needs to be done if our organizations are going to honor the kingdom we seek to make a reality . . . on earth as it is in heaven."

STEVEN G. W. MOORE, executive director, The M. J. Murdock Charitable Trust

Handbook for
BATTERED
LEADERS

Janis Bragan Balda

Wesley D. Balda

IVP Books

An imprint of InterVarsity Press
Downers Grove, Illinois

InterVarsity Press
P.O. Box 1400, Downers Grove, IL 60515-1426
World Wide Web: www.ivpress.com
Email: email@ivpress.com

InterVarsity Press® is the book-publishing division of InterVarsity Christian Fellowship/USA®, a movement of students and faculty active on campus at hundreds of universities, colleges and schools of nursing in the United States of America, and a member movement of the International Fellowship of Evangelical Students. For information about local and regional activities, write Public Relations Dept., InterVarsity Christian Fellowship/USA, 6400 Schroeder Rd., P.O. Box 7895, Madison, WI 53707-7895, or visit the IVCF website at <www.intervarsity.org>.

Scripture quotations, unless otherwise noted, are from The Message. *Copyright © 1993, 1994, 1995. Used by permission of NavPress Publishing Group. All rights reserved.*

Jim Wallis, "The Power of Reconciliation," reprinted with permission from Sojourners, 1-800-714-7474, www.sojo.net.

While all stories in this book are true, some names and identifying information in this book have been changed to protect the privacy of the individuals involved.

Interior design: Beth Hagenberg

ISBN 978-0-8308-5678-7

Printed in the United States of America ∞

Library of Congress Cataloging-in-Publication Data
A catalog record for this book is available from the Library of Congress.

P	19	18	17	16	15	14	13	12	11	10	9	8	7	6	5	4	3	2	1
Y	29	28	27	26	25	24	23	22	21	20	19	18	17	16	15	14	13			

To our children,

Sam, Joanna and Andy,

Daniel and Lisa, Erica and Lenny,

and their children,

who bring us love and hope

Contents

1

If You Haven't Bled,
You Haven't Led

You can safely assume you've remade God in your own image
when it turns out God hates the same people you do.

ANNE LAMOTT, *BIRD BY BIRD*

Most of the best leaders and managers we know are or have been battered.[1] We realized this some time ago, while teaching an MBA course in Brazil. Bullying, gossiping, mobbing, blaming, harassing, falsely accusing, impugning or even ignoring—all these and more are common experiences for people we've known in leadership roles.

The apostle Paul himself was a battered leader. This became clear to us as we read his second letter to the Corinthian church:

> You should have been . . . sticking up for me and commending me instead of making me do it for myself. You know from personal experience that even if I'm a nobody, a nothing, I wasn't second-rate compared to those big-shot apostles you're so taken with. All the signs that mark

a true apostle were in evidence while I was with you through both good times and bad: signs of portent, signs of wonder, signs of power. Did you get less of me or of God than any of the other churches? The only thing you got less of was less responsibility for my upkeep. Well, I'm sorry. Forgive me for depriving you. (2 Corinthians 12:11-13)

Paul's experience resembles the hardship that so many leaders experience in a community beset by change and crisis. And he had some profound thoughts on the subject. Eugene Peterson's introduction to the letter puts the harsh light of day on the church: "For anyone operating under the naïve presumption that joining a Christian church is a good way to meet all the best people and cultivate smooth social relations, a reading of Paul's Corinthian correspondence is the prescribed cure."[2] Peterson identifies the central theme of 2 Corinthians as resistance to Paul's leadership—the Corinthians "accused him of inconsistencies, impugned his motives, questioned his credentials. They didn't argue with what he had written; they simply denied his right to tell them what to do."[3]

Rarely do we face a situation of change or crisis where complicated layers of relationships and expectations are not contributing factors. Battered leaders may range from completely innocent victims to managers who have some (even much) culpability in creating their own pain. Second Corinthians explores a range of causes of, implications from, and reactions to crisis. It develops the theme of *broken trust*—not by Paul, despite the congregation's assertions, but instead by those he nurtured. Paul recognizes that outcomes are negatively multiplied when trust is betrayed, particularly at the deepest spiritual levels. The kind of trust we develop as members of a faith community—its extent, durability and expansiveness—translates to a level of vulnerability with each other. For Paul, the intensity of his commitment to the community meant the sharing of a deep and vulnerable trust. Here he explores the horrific consequences when trust at this level is broken.

Paul also explores the nature of *toxic leadership*. It is tempting and convenient to suspect the leader first when conflict festers. Yet in some cases it is the followers who are at fault. Second Corinthians triumphs partly because it identifies the phenomenon of toxic followers for leaders who are used to blaming themselves or taking on the blame their followers assign them. Followers can batter leaders all on their own, or they can be encouraged in dysfunction by others who have influence and power.

The third area where leaders are battered, after taking hits from those above and those who follow them, is that more nameless but overarching threat, *the system itself.* The damage attributable to the system by relationship-stifling bureaucracy or unidentifiable but injury-creating processes ranges from simple obfuscation to the swamps of principalities and powers. Paul is well aware of the works and ways of evil; he notes at several points in the dialogue where systemic and impersonal powers create pain for the leader.

We are amazed by how quickly executives we work with or people in our management classes can identify the toxic followers in their lives and how frequently they want to elaborate on the circumstances. The managers and leaders we talk to invariably confess to having felt like a battered leader at some point in their careers. One executive recalled that "most of the best people I know used to work at _____," a painful indictment of this organization's competence in eliminating managers and creating a cadre of battered leaders. Others have observed, "If you're not battered, you haven't led."

There are very few pure situations where the leader, the followers or the system are specifically, entirely and absolutely to blame in a failed community or enterprise. We all contribute, as occupants of a broken world, to the complexities in our organizations that hurt and disrupt. At the same time, we leaders sometimes take on blame we shouldn't, especially those of us with shame-driven upbringings, who have received from well-meaning caregivers a large dosage of guilt. This overhanging cloud blocks breakthroughs in settling organizational issues. Leaders over-assign fault to themselves—which can be conveniently reinforced by followers—which then stalls the situation until a new cycle renews the downward trend or something breaks the cycle. Peter Senge calls these *reinforcing loops*, which can resemble vicious circles with infinite iterations. Resolution appears only when something or someone intervenes to break the cycle. For apprentices of Jesus, this "break" should take the form of reconvening around common ground with humility and forgiveness.

Believing that leadership is a critical factor for any manager or executive and that all truth is God's truth, we thought that a leader as wise as Paul might have some mature insights to share with us. This study is designed to be a tool for leaders who have been beaten up while leading and serving their followers. It will provide some practices, as well as concepts for self-awareness and reengaging in the business purpose or organizational mission, when faced with bullying bosses, toxic followers and recalcitrant systems.

THE CORINTHIAN CASE

Business schools all over the world long ago captured the value of using stories to teach business and management concepts.

The Harvard Business School employs the Harvard Case Method. Management professor and writer Peter Drucker used short cases as teaching tools for decades. We see cleverly embedded within 2 Corinthians a classic management case study, with a first-person account of how one leader handled a distressing organizational problem that had serious personal implications. This case study gives us a sweeping view of conflict resolution, leadership and power (and in some cases, leading *without* power), emotional intelligence, negotiation, organizational life cycles and leadership communication—common to all institutions—in addition to problems unique to Christian organizations. This approach forms the wider discussion in the chapters that follow, beginning with the leader's account of the situation or case.

A good business case should be true, though identities of players can be masked if anonymity is needed. Usually, cases tell the stories of familiar companies and their challenges, and are structured to raise the key issues in a situation requiring decisions and resolution. The student prepares the case through individual analysis, possibly exploring it with a small group beforehand, and then discusses it in class or among the team, often with supplementary materials or even a speaker from the company involved. Generalization about the issues and processes wraps up the learning process. There is nearly always a protagonist through whose eyes the scenario is viewed.

Cases emphasize *metaphors* and *simulation*. The metaphor captures different forms of meaning about the case, and simulation requires the student to act through processes and solutions as if actually living in the situation. Here are questions the student can ask in preparing the case:

- Who is the decision maker (protagonist)?
- What are the decision maker's objectives (agendas)?
- What decisions need to be made?
- If I were the decision maker (simulation) what problems, opportunities and risks would I face?
- Do I have evidence to use in making the decision? Is this evidence any good? Is there more data? (Most difficult leadership decisions do not have enough data—that is why the leader must make them. If they were easy anyone could decide!)
- What are my alternative courses of action?
- How will I assess the alternatives?
- What should I do?
- How do I convince others that this is the right decision?
- What did I learn?
- How does it relate to other situations and to my own experience?[4]

With this approach, you can see how putting ourselves in Paul's place and trying to figure out this Corinthian dilemma can help us learn. We could consider this letter a long and rambling memo from a highly relational senior executive who is close to his people, addressing issues in a branch office close to full collapse; or the founder of a national nonprofit responding to challenges of a local chapter being heavily influenced by individuals with seemingly related but actually conflicting goals and methodologies. In this book we are asking you to treat Paul's document as a management case study. This will require shifting some paradigms and the use of several innovations in order to learn from 2 Corinthians.

First, we are using Eugene Peterson's retelling of faith stories, published as *The Message*. Sometimes when studying something familiar, it is a good idea to shift our paradigm. Serious students of Christianity can get complacent about the Bible; the familiar phrases that bring us comfort also lull us into modes of listening to God that limit the imagination and creativity of his messages to us. If you are a regular reader of the Bible, try reading through 2 Corinthians in the Bible translation that you use most often, and you might notice how quickly you become distracted or preoccupied or expect that you know what is coming next. Unless we reframe the message, we often drift into mindless distraction rather than mindful attentiveness. It is like ADHD for the soul—endlessly wandering through spiritual rabbit trails that diminish our effectiveness as disciples.

By providing a new context for the central message of a text from the Bible, we can find application to our everyday world. At the same time, we must handle the Word accurately and rightly. There is a good reason why preachers spend years in theological education and reflection. Though the Spirit guides us into truth, exegesis, hermeneutics, classical languages, history and the various theologies—biblical, systematic, historical and so on—are useful tools along the way. No reputable theologian would use highly sophisticated exegetical tools to figure out *Veggie Tales*. Everyone understands it is a different genre that brings new understandings, but within agreed-upon constraints and limitations.

Peterson never intended his *Message* translation of the Bible to be a technical rendition incorporating the latest textual criticism with pure grammatical interpretations from the original languages. If you have glanced through portions of *The Message*, you realize that you are reading modern North American phrases, complete with colloquialisms, slang, and contemporary metaphors. No attempt is made to sensitize the language to fit into every cultural situation. Just as a young person who watches a television program produced in Los Angeles or New York can understand basically everything going on, so too with Peterson's *The Message*, an individual with a decent understanding of English from anywhere in the world will understand these chapters at once. It is *dynamically equivalent.*

There are other creative avenues available to explore this idea of returning to the text in counterintuitive ways. So-called red-letter editions of the Gospels seem rather old-fashioned, but they can be compelling. Try reading through a Gospel, disregarding everything but the specific words of Jesus (printed in red), taking these in sequence through the chapters and verses. If you have not realized it before, you will see that the content is radical. Jesus' words can be hard, direct and unequivocal. For another example, read through Acts, finding where the various speakers present the gospel, and copy on a separate piece of paper *only those phrases in quotation marks.* You will see how simple and straightforward the gospel message is, as preached to first-century listeners: Jesus was the Messiah as foretold to the Jews; he came as a man, was tortured to death but overcame death, coming back fully alive yet transformed; we knew him and touched him with our own hands; repent! That is about it in terms of the central message.

In this book we are not attempting to address every issue raised in 2 Corinthians. We focus instead on highlighting certain leadership areas that seem to trouble many of us in organizations. Business case studies can be written to emphasize certain issues in a situation and are not intended to encompass every complexity the scenario presents. Most good historians recognize that the full truth of any event may not ever be ultimately grasped and that we all should learn to apply thoughtful approaches when considering history. In the same way, a business case does not aim to disclose the full truth of a situation, if that were even possible, but to address specific issues. One professor may emphasize different themes than another professor, yet both are teaching the same case. We face similar challenges in understanding Scripture, even when using traditional approaches. And, of course, the Holy Spirit chooses with sovereignty to make the Logos alive in new ways, depending on the context.

We work iteratively back and forth from the text, without inductively seeking to draw out every theme. In the same way, some themes are introduced that are not directly traceable to a specific situation Paul faced, yet are important to organizational leaders. For example, the problems in the case are framed entirely by Paul's take on the Corinthians—where Paul views himself as innocent rather than as a sinful participant in their issues. Yet in many of the organizational scenarios we face, our own behaviors may have played a significant part in the unfolding of our corporate dramas. We address these because the factors involved are important to consider, even though Paul did not specifically address them.

A third innovation requires that we allow *Saint* Paul to step down off his pedestal and speak as a fellow manager/leader. Jesus certainly invites us, out of his humanity, to share both his joys and sufferings. And though Jesus was without sin, Paul would be the first to tell us his own struggles and claim his place beside us as both colleague and sinner.

This requires accepting Paul's sarcasm—it is there at times— and to read between the lines in some sections. Though this might be considered an argument from silence, what Paul frequently does *not* say is as important as what he does say. For example, certain implications can be inferred from Paul's positive admonitions to the dysfunctional team at Corinth. If Paul extols the virtues, for example, of telling the truth in love, then it is reasonable to infer that there was some lying going on. For those hearers who have been lying, the statement will convict, and the proverbial shoe will fit and will therefore have to be worn.

Invariably, your own situations will come to mind. Whether your fact situation precisely matches a scriptural example or not is unimportant. Each of us can reflect on all the possibilities the text suggests—not responding with rigid scriptural frameworks. Allow your God-inspired imagination to work out solutions with all the tools at hand. It will help to remind yourself that we are treating this as a management situation—shift your paradigm from the first century to the present and reflect on how little some things have changed!

DISTINCTIVES OF 2 CORINTHIANS

One of the most amazing things about this case study is that it was written two thousand years ago. So we may read the biblical text with a kind of artificial reverence or alternatively view it as less than inspired—both perspectives miss the subtleties and practical learning it contains. The former attitude is evident in several of the commentaries, including some that exalt Paul to the level of superhuman action hero. In fact, he can be sarcastic, empathetic, slightly devious, disingenuous, humble, ironic, arrogant or deeply affirming. In other words, he is completely human, a lot like us, while also serving as an example to us as we learn to manage and lead better.

But this is not a straightforward letter with one clear level of meaning. There is much that is going on between the lines. Paul constantly keeps his readers in Corinth off balance. There is a prophetic sense to Paul's words at times. In one sense it may be *proleptic*, in that Paul is speaking a future truth into reality, perhaps in part reflecting a kingdom theology. At other times the subtle give and take of a well-trained legal mind speaks out of the pages, pushing and prodding.

Sometimes Paul writes in a particular way to make a point. For example, at 2 Corinthians 13:1 he properly cites that two or three witnesses should give evidence; he then proceeds to assert that he can be all three witnesses—one person speaking, just on three different occasions!

A caveat is necessary here. Although it may be a popular tendency, slavishly applying the ideas and teachings of Scripture directly to organizational situations is not always a good idea. Treating Jesus as chief executive officer of a company or framing the Jerusalem elders as a nonprofit board of directors again suggests arguments from silence, past a certain point. The current trend lauding servant leadership faces similar exegetical perils. The phrase is catchy, but its application is much more complex than is often considered.

In the same sense theologians caution us not to treat New Testament parables as sophisticated didactic tools, but rather to ferret out an initial simple teaching from their context, antecedents, cultural dimensions and contemporary perceptions. New Testament writers would no doubt have been a little baffled by some modern doctoral dissertations attempting to explain a simple teaching in nine hundred pages or more. Conceding that Paul's apostolic authority may not quite be the same mandate we are given in an organizational situation is helpful in applying the actual lessons of 2 Corinthians. We cannot necessarily handle our own dilemmas in exactly the same way Paul did. In fact, the need for organizationally and culturally adaptive paradigms in addressing these complex situations is one of the critical management lessons we must learn. The complexity creates situational dynamics where there is no simple or single answer. By studying 2 Corinthians and Paul's handling of his situation, however, we gain insights into management tasks and practices that can help us discern and identify problem areas and seek solutions that are effective yet personal. This is the search for simplicity on the other side of complexity.

Contemplating 2 Corinthians as a case study draws us into thinking about leadership, but as a *management* case study we are challenged to press further in, think more critically, and confront day-to-day practice. Most, if not all, of the topics we talk about in this book link to concepts in the management world that we can use for "benchmarking" or "good/best practices." The management and leadership concepts Paul applies flow out of his own benchmarking process for his particular thorny organizational problems. We frame leadership as a *dimension* of management; management itself is the overall task of *making knowledge effective through relationships*—invariably in organizations.

Leadership

All of us manage. If we are executives of some sort in organizations or businesses, we manage our direct reports. But we also manage personal finances, our Girl Scout troop, our bosses, our families, ourselves. Everyone is a manager of some sort. To do this we use many dimensions of management.

An early twentieth-century writer initially identified the dimensions of management as *planning, organizing, leading* and *controlling*.⁵ We could add more—networking, communicating, liaising, staffing and so on. Leading—and, of course, leadership—is therefore one of the things we do at certain times as a dimension within the larger task of managing.

We propose that leading and leadership happen when traditional or commonly understood power and authority are not available or do not apply. Max De Pree's book *Leading Without Power* is aptly named: we *lead* in those situations when we cannot (or should not) simply tell an individual or group what to do, based on our position, role or responsibility—when we have no *structural power*. When the person who takes on the responsibility for the task does not possess marginally more power in the situation than the others and so cannot use it to move the others along, there is little or no power differential. Some other means of persuading or influencing others to carry out a task or produce a result are needed.

In a helpful discussion in his book *Good to Great and the Social Sectors*, Jim Collins speaks of executive and legislative leadership.⁶ (This is discussed in further detail in chapter two.) He characterizes the CEO who has enough structural power to make decisions alone as *executive* leadership. In situations of complex governance and diffuse power structures, however, the senior leader does not have the structural power to make decisions alone, creating a situation of *legislative* leadership. Legislative leadership may corroborate the theory that leadership emerges as the power differential approaches zero. Building on Collins's idea, the two could be conceived of as a continuum, with pure executive leadership at one end and equally pure legislative leadership at the other.

Pure executive leadership (power differential = 100)	Pure legislative leadership (power differential = 0)

The ultimate executive leader might be an army general, possessing significant structural power, requiring unswerving obedience—one person wielding a great deal of authority, able to call dramatic action into being with a word. At the other end of the continuum, the resistance of one principled (or unprincipled) individual completely without structural power can bring an entire organization to a standstill. Perhaps a Quaker gathering could exemplify the purest form of this, where everything can stop based on a matter of principle (versus preference). In between lie an infinite number of variations of organizational leadership, both positive and negative. Organizations do not remain static along the continuum; circumstances and individuals shift their positions and the shape of transactions and decisions made.

Power

Power—the means to manage that comes with the position or responsibility—is initially a neutral term and can end up being legitimate or illegitimate. Not only managers but followers can exercise power, either legitimately or illegitimately. A major premise of this book is that followers can use power inappropriately and illegitimately to batter their leaders.

Apostles and other innovators, by their very job description, do a lot of managing in all the same areas we have described above. When the *power differential* is zero or close to it, leadership is needed to manage. For various reasons, we find Paul effectively at a power differential of zero in Corinth, even though he was the founder of the group. As Eugene Peterson notes, his followers have simply denied him the right to tell them what to do. From Paul's perspective, not only is the power differential at zero, the battering quotient is climbing quickly. These people have gotten negative about the whole affair.

Paul must now exercise leadership in its purest sense. It is the only dimension of management that can get the Corinthian program back on track. He is effectively powerless, certainly from the perspective of the Corinthians, because at least at one stage in their relationship they have withdrawn and denied his right to lead.

Daniel Goleman's work on emotional intelligence resonates with Paul's responses in the case study. Goleman identifies social and emotional "competencies" that are particularly necessary in zero power differential situations, including emotional self-awareness, an achievement orientation, adaptability, emotional self-control, a positive outlook, empathy, organizational awareness, conflict management, coaching and mentoring, influence, inspirational leadership, and teamwork.[7] Leadership scholar Jean Lipman-Blumen's descriptions of various leadership styles—direct, relational and instrumental facets—also offer insights into the way people use their strengths and personalities to relate to those they lead. (These will be discussed later.) People exercising leadership can combine connective leadership styles and social or emotional competencies to obtain the results they need. We will see that Paul is a master at this.

AUTHORITY

Paul's authority among the Corinthian Christians is that of both founder and apostle. In organizations, whether for-profit or social sector, the founder occupies a special place, in some cases possessing "apostolic" status. Part of Paul's appeal for obedience flows from his role as "father" of this particular community. The dialogue gets parental at times, with undertones of raising an adolescent. And if being founder was not enough, Paul claims further to be an *apostle*, a word commonly used for someone sent forth or sent out as an emissary. It is the title attributed to the twelve disciples of Jesus Christ; though not one of the Twelve, Paul considered himself to have been appointed as an apostle by the resurrected Jesus who appeared to him in a vision. (He refers to himself as the apostle to the Gentiles in Romans 11:13.)

It may be helpful to understand that the "founders" of the community of Jesus (the reconstituted Twelve plus Paul and a few others) are not perceived in quite the same way as some modern-day apostles. While it may be true that apostolic ministries and roles continue, those thirteen clearly wielded a different kind of authority. Even the two thousand years of claims to authority of the Roman papacy are baseless without Peter, one of the Twelve and considered the rock on whom Jesus built his church.

Paul repeatedly calls attention to the place of high visibility from which he speaks: "We stand in Christ's presence when we speak; God looks us in the face. We get what we say straight from God and say it as honestly as we can" (2 Corinthians 2:17). This is unique positioning that buttresses Paul's authority as founder, apostle and member of the inner circle. It is reminiscent of Jesus in John 14 claiming to do only what he sees the Father doing. It is special authority and not necessarily available to the rest of us. It highlights the problem of simplistic application of organizational situations in Scripture to all of life. Yet we will see how this role makes little difference to the Corinthians as they seek to assert their right to manage their own situation and choose whom they will follow.

PAUL'S LEADERSHIP STRATEGY

Paul understood that though the authority and power of the risen Christ stood behind him, resolution of the Corinthian crisis required subtlety, persuasion and communication. The community at Corinth grew from the early efforts of a mobile mission community traveling around a large region, planting branches of the Christian movement in various places. This mission community (Paul's team) emerged from a well-established base community in Jerusalem but operated largely on its own because time and distance necessitated it. A combination of poor local leadership, toxic followers, cultural complexities, and unsustainable practices and systems ignited a crisis of survival for this faltering group, however. The situation deteriorated to the extent that cordial relationships and sensible dialogue were no longer possible. Having been denied the right to lead this group, Paul steps back, as any astute management guru would do, to assess the leadership challenge using the most effective method he could, while writing from a distance.

In a masterful restatement, Paul shifts the context to one of his own choosing. Recognizing he no longer possesses the authority, at least in the eyes of the Corinthians, to tell them what to do in a traditional sense, he creates a community of practice in response to the crisis and orients it around new tasks to shift the focus to mission. On the way, he identifies the destructive individuals and forces generating the problems and sidelines them. He shapes the community by a compelling appeal to the deeper needs of others, moving the emphasis to external results. When he lays out the ground rules, he is not actually being heavy-handed, because the moral and ethical demands of these ground rules were there from the beginning, clear and unequivocal. He simply redesigns the rules of engagement with the community.

Admittedly, we are speculating here, but this is allowed when exploring management case studies. From an organizational standpoint, this community would eventually have to be re-established. In the biblical record we are not told how this happens. The absence of power in a community of practice provides a certain fundamental strength, but the congregation, like other forms of organization that evolve out of crisis, requires a strengthened form of leadership. The Corinthians should have no doubts that they are in a crisis. And it is in this sense of urgency that Paul wades in to realign this fragmented group.

PART ONE

TOXIC LEADERS, FOLLOWERS, SYSTEMS

2

The Leadership Conundrum

Over the years, the pathos and pain we have observed in victims of so-called Christian organizations, whether structured specifically as churches or taking other organizational forms, buttresses Peterson's insight from our first chapter: "For anyone operating under the naïve presumption that joining a Christian church is a good way to meet all the best people and cultivate smooth social relations, a reading of Paul's Corinthian correspondence is the prescribed cure."[1]

However, before addressing the complexities of organizations, we need to understand the battered leader as victim in three frames of reference:

Toxic leaders. If those who lead you are toxic, they are fully capable of creating hostile organizations completely on their own, by being bullies or by failing to act or by encouraging followers to develop questionable organizational behaviors.

Toxic followers. When toxic followers reach critical mass, they can use techniques such as conspiracies, back channeling, triangulation and mobbing to waylay the best leaders.

Toxic systems. Finally, the system itself—embracing culture, history, policy, corporate memory and other factors—can provide scenarios ranging from innovation and soul-killing bogs to classic principalities and powers. The faceless system can kill leaders just as usefully as bad bosses and noxious subordinates.

Toxic Leaders

Working for an oppressive, vindictive, threatening, bullying or cruel boss provides an easy-to-understand picture of why some leaders are battered.[2] Identifying other bad leaders is an easy task. The leadership book business has never been more booming or profitable, and most talk about good leaders. Some authors are exploring bad leadership with good results. The best study yet can be found in Jean Lipman-Blumen's *The Allure of Toxic Leaders*. She capably discusses bad leaders but goes one important step further: she suggests that we don't have to tolerate these bad leaders, and she offers direction for how we can survive them:

> Toxic leaders leave their followers worse off than they found them, sometimes even eliminating—by undermining, firing, disenfranchising, imprisoning, incapacitating, torturing, or even killing—many of their own people.
>
> They consciously feed their followers reassuring illusions that enhance their own power and impair the followers' capacity to act independently (e.g., by persuading followers that only the leader has the appropriate answers).
>
> Toxic leaders subvert those structures and processes intended to generate truth and excellence. They undermine civil liberties and due process through authoritarian initiatives, including informally or formally stifling criticism and teaching followers (sometimes by intimidation and authoritarianism) to comply with the leader's directives.
>
> They play to the followers' basest fears and needs, even

misleading them through deliberate misdiagnoses of problems. Sometimes, they treat their own followers well, but persuade them to hate and/or destroy others.

Some toxic leaders maliciously set their followers not only against outsiders but also against one another. They maintain power through intimidation and terror and resort to scapegoating the weak and the despised.

At times, toxic leaders display their addiction to power by using improper means to cling to it.

They often weaken the legal processes for selecting and supporting new leaders.

They fail to nurture other leaders, including their own successors (with the occasional exception of blood kin), by building totalitarian or narrowly dynastic regimes.

At the lower end of toxicity, leaders ignore or promote incompetence and corruption. They fail to understand the nature of relevant problems and consistently perform ineffectively in leadership situations.[3]

As Dee Hock, founder of Visa, observes, "True power is never used. If you use power, you never really had it."

Over her career, Astrid had left a number of positions under similar circumstances. Each time strong performance and significant contribution preceded her eventual conflict and deteriorating relationship with a boss. Her supervisors were quick to point out her flaws, to frame and control the dialogue (to the extent that any existed), and eventually would "weary" her out of the position.[4] The organization would turn a blind eye to such internal attacks. In several cases where she resigned, it was from the pressure of imminent termination or from workplace bullying, both resulting in emotional abuse.

Astrid developed guilt that grew over her decades of employment at various places. Her perception was that she was flawed, incapable of working with others and doomed never to break the cycle. In nearly every situation, however, Astrid was generally well liked, with subordinates who were loyal and supportive. Although she had a strong personality (originally seen as a plus for her position), her creative and sometimes aggressive style was not enough to explain this negative reinforcing loop. Digging deeper, it became clear that conflict within her staff traced back to inappropriate back channeling by the toxic leader involving her subordinates. Each boss, it turned out, was a toxic leader, invariably exhibiting low emotional intelligence, intent on exercising power and control, and allowing dysfunctional behavior in order to create results.

The answer emerged not so much because Astrid tended to attract these kind of bosses—or in some sense was intuitively choosing incompetent supervisors to create havoc in her life—but rather because of her morally driven intolerance of toxic leadership. Her character was so sensitized to bad leadership that her integrity triumphed each time in the end. Astrid needed to change her self-perception from the negative (as a job-hopper) to the positive: she was someone with a high awareness of supervisory toxicity.

> Paul alludes to toxic leaders in several ways throughout 2 Corinthians. He specifically describes actual individuals and their behaviors. He identifies more general behaviors without explicitly linking to others who have influenced the Corinthians. Finally, by singling out positive leadership traits, he indirectly labels still other toxic behaviors.

The multiple incidences of toxic leaders Astrid worked for indicates how pervasive this phenomenon is. For most of us, Lipman-Blumen's challenging question, "Why do we tolerate and follow toxic leaders?" becomes too painful to confront. Our fear of losing income, reputation or self-esteem edges us into compromises that damage our hearts and souls. We are willing to bear these burdens and accept these scars because the alternatives frighten us too much. How can I sacrifice my family's well-being or feed my children if I'm constantly marching away from positions that upset my fragile moral frame of reference? Life is hard, so I just need to put up with my bullying boss . . . right?

The logical extension of the theory emerging from Astrid's experience leads to a possibly startling conclusion: many leaders suffer from some degree of toxicity. It wasn't Astrid's problem; it was her supervisors' issues. But in their toxicity, her bosses delegated the guilt to Astrid. If any part of our religious position recognizes fallenness—original sin or evil in the world—then we understand that leadership, grounded by power, has potentially toxic roots. This is not such a bad theory because it gives us a clear starting point for identifying and surviving toxic leadership, both as leader and as led.

Toxicity manifests in numerous and pungent ways—bullying, toxic ambivalence, pretension, fantasy and hypocrisy.

BULLYING AND COMMANDING

Bullying involves things like unfair treatment, public humiliation and other forms of threatening behavior. While some bullying is straightforward, other behaviors can be subtler yet still create toxicity. These include undermining one's position or responsibility, falsely taking credit, spreading rumors and half-truths, and social ostracism.

Some research identifies bullying as an epidemic, especially in the workplace. For example, in the United States over a third of the workforce may have been bullied. The practice can be a form of same-gender/same-race harassment not covered by numerous laws and judgments of recent years. Nearly three-fourths of bullies are bosses.[5] This, of course, makes it a leadership issue.

Whenever a leader commands, the power dynamic shifts and can become problematic. There is a thin line between commanding and bullying. In a classic management article, John French and Bertram Raven suggest the background for the practice of commanding and related problems. They identify five forms of power—coercive, reward, legitimate, referent and expert. Commanding smacks of coercive, though variations of the others can also wrong followers.[6]

Bullying has been defined as "offensive, abusive, intimidating, malicious or insulting behavior, often amounting to an abuse of power, position or knowledge to humiliate a subordinate or colleague."[7] Bullying can involve shouting, swearing, name-calling, malicious sarcasm, threats to safety, or actions that are threatening, intimidating, humiliating, hostile, offensive or cruel. To cement their position, bullies evaluate performance unfairly, deny advancement, steal credit, attack reputations, give arbitrary instruction, and even assign unsafe work. They can interfere, sabotage, undermine, and encourage failure.[8] One respondent recalls a senior leader who acted coercively and bullied rather than commanded. Invariably, one-on-one meetings held by this leader took place behind closed doors. The respondent would be called into his office, and the leader would close the door and shout, "I'm your boss—just do what I tell you to do!" That the situation had degraded to this point reflected the leader's incompetence rather than the follower's issues.

The underlying phenomenon often identified as workplace bullying can result in physical as well as emotional and psychological disorders, including a diagnosis such as post-traumatic stress disorder.

> For Paul the key to comparing himself as the true apostle to the toxic false apostles lies in the signs, wonders and miracles he performed (2 Corinthians 12:12 NIV). Other than this section, however, he makes no further appeal to signs, wonders and miracles. In fact, his remaining discussion reveals a potent leadership toolkit of a more garden variety of valid and applicable management responses.
>
> For example, the true leader acts with "integrity and godly sincerity" (1:12 NIV), presenting himself as a "servant for Jesus' sake" (4:5 NIV, recalling collaborative approaches, without using power), and perhaps as an "ambassador" (5:20 NIV).
>
> At the same time, the true leader makes judgments about what is best (8:10), champions equality and equity (8:13), is zealous (8:22), and takes the role of "co-worker" (8:23 NIV).
>
> In situations where we as leaders may not necessarily be able to point to our own instances of signs, wonders and miracles for validation, the authentic, courageous, and morally good and right actions on our part constitute a basis.

Toxic Ambivalence: Sins of Omission

We can probably agree that toxic leadership does not necessarily require intentionality—it can be accomplished quite effectively as a sin of omission rather than commission. Simple ineptness and rank incompetence breed toxicity in their own way. The Peter Principle—"in a hierarchy every employee tends to rise to his level of incompetence," or "maximum incompetence" in some versions—has been shown to have statistical validity.[9] Followers experience frustration where managers do nothing. Blocking the movement of others in a forward direction by rigid adherence to outdated or ineffective policies, or failing to offer management support to valid projects—for no reason other than to serve their own egos or fears—is debilitating and destructive. Often at the center of such action is the unspoken but often recognizable tenet that the leader's self-interest dominates any and all decisions.

Steven Sample, former president of the University of Southern California, describes "thinking gray" as an attribute of a contrarian leader.[10] It refers to avoiding, delaying or deferring a decision until it has to be made, which really is a decision in itself. In some highly charged political situations the leader may walk a thin line between pragmatic indecision and toxic ambivalence. While this may preserve college presidencies or other newly installed senior leaders, it can also be a quick route to toxic ambivalence.

Pretension: The Problem of Celebrity

"As soon as enough people give you enough compliments and you're wielding more power than you've ever had in your life, it's not that you become . . . arrogant . . . or become rude to people, but you get a false sense of your own importance and what you've accomplished. You actually think you've altered the course of history."[11]

The fact that this quote came from a movie star, Leonardo DiCaprio, rather than an executive only amplifies its relevance. Characterizing the leader as celebrity may sound like an odd take, but we can see how aptly it fits. Through a variety of circumstances any public event (physical, virtual or broadcasted), we create celebrity. It is a form of leadership that emerges from visibility and branding. A name becomes increasingly recognizable, and a set of meanings is attached to it.[12] There can then be a subtle shift, as a normal human being becomes a brand. Meaning becomes larger or different for the person involved: a famous author exercises leadership through ideas; a famous actress leverages great facial bone structure; a famous speaker communicates charismatically with a deep voice and theatrical gestures. In the broadest sense of leadership, each leads and each faces the challenge of celebrity, even if only on a local scale. (For a worst-case scenario consider recent reality shows.)

Our beliefs and resulting behaviors are essential to who we are. Celebrity status can alter our circumstances or the individuals outside our control, creating situations in opposition to our personal wishes and beyond our maturity.[13] This leads to unintended consequences of our leadership actions. Uncritical followers, attracted by the brand, ignore a host of warning signs.

> Paul painfully deals with toxic leaders ("big-shot apostles" or "pseudo-apostles") who are acting out all the worst implications of celebrity as he confronts individuals who follow such people slavishly. Not only do they favor the trappings of celebrity status, but they fault Paul for his unwillingness to engage as a leader in the same way (11:4-6, 12-15).

A foundational indicator of toxic celebrity is a lack of accountability. If you watch the entertainment news of the day, you may be familiar with the concept of *entourage*. It may not be a shock that these are people kept around for their very ability to say yes to the leader's every request. Leaders enthralled with celebrity are literally "in thrall" to the unholy freedom to do exactly whatever feels good at the moment. This is the dark side of celebrity, clarified by Leonardo DiCaprio above. At the same time, in view of the special status they are afforded, celebrities are placed under extraordinary pressure without the benefit of being held responsible for results. Those followers who are eventually disappointed or hurt are also usually the ones who bring down celebrities once they discover their feet of clay.

Technology can amplify or alter meaning in surprising ways. At the most basic level a set of large speakers is necessary for a rock band to gain celebrity status. (There may be a few singers out there still functioning as celebrities without using electricity in some way, but we are not aware of them!) Television and Internet technologies amplify meaning and magnify face and name recognition, thereby expanding brand value. The stories of how popular social technology forums such as blogs or Twitter have quickly thrust individuals into prominence and brought others down is an everyday occurrence.

The phenomenon is not limited to Hollywood stars. Some leaders consciously leverage a personal brand to be more effective, giving little thought to the moral or ethical implications of their burgeoning celebrity. Many can be found eventually swinging in the wind, riding the wave of their fame in the salacious tabloid press at the logical end of this quest. These leaders represent a fair and balanced cross section of politicians, corporate executives and preachers.

Observers of celebrities move from natural skepticism to trust and, therefore, "followership." The celebrity exercises leadership through an increasingly assumed (and artificial) credibility. Observers become followers by buying into this credibility, essentially trusting an image created and amplified by technology, made meaningful by an evolving brand (whether well managed or not), as the following crowd grows and sometimes even goes viral.

To varying degrees we all want to be celebrities because it means others are impressed by what we say, do things for us, affirm us, become our "friends," don't criticize or hurt us, and primarily allow us to exercise power over them—only because we are important, not because we are right. That is the bad news.

Because celebrity is a form of leadership, it can become toxic. But in and of itself, celebrity is not bad. We start with a neutral concept and by understanding it attempt to deal with its realities. If leaders are defined as those with followers, then anyone with one or more followers will deal with some aspect of celebrity as we are defining it.

Celebrity in this generic sense is going to happen to leaders with visibility, whether desired or not, so how do we keep it from getting toxic? Toxic celebrities are generally humorless about their own shortcomings, travel with uncritical followers, seek more celebrity and constantly build their own brands. Their celebrity can turn into notoriety when toxicity becomes public. However, these celebrity leaders may also remain effective (as they define it) or even become more effective in inappropriate ways.

The bottom line is that celebrity without community is toxic. Community, in some sense, provides accountability and prevents toxicity, if understood properly. But what kind of community? A group of mere followers, an acquiescent community, does not exercise accountability. The only community of any worth is a community of loving detractors.

One of Max De Pree's most memorable quotes is, "The first responsibility of a leader is to define reality."[14] The idea of defining reality as the initial responsibility of the leader is a powerful concept. But note that defining reality is a *responsibility* of the leader—not a prerogative! Those who cite De Pree often slip past this part toward toxicity. We recall certain gleeful approaches to defining reality when leaders took over and acted more like they were cleaning house (which can be a form of bullying). A clean sweep through an organization when uncalled for can be just as toxic as inaction or ambivalence when deep change is needed. That is perhaps why in continuing his response, De Pree expands the phrase by adding, "The last [responsibility] is to say thank you. In between the two, the leader must become a servant and a debtor."[15] These concepts are complex and tricky, but at a minimum they require that the leader always put the interests of the other—the health and tone of the "body"—over his self-interest, even when defining reality involves change management.

Hypocrisy: the Problem of the Servant Leader

A catchy aphorism is a wonderful thing. Augustine's "love the sinner and hate the sin" and Yogi Berra's "when you get to a fork in the road, take it" anchor both ends of using language creatively.

The phrase "servant leadership" in the lively history of aphorisms and clichés may too have taken on a life of its own with much enthusiasm and perhaps slightly less critical thought. As a result, we have a duty not to dismiss it, but rather to approach it in its common understanding within the practice of management and leadership. Robert Greenleaf is well known for his development of the concept,[16] but a host of other authors are adding to the corpus. Jesus' counterintuitive teaching on servant leadership reputedly launched the movement (or at least gets cited often):

> You know that the rulers of the Gentiles lord it over them, and their high officials exercise authority over

them. Not so with you. Instead, whoever wants to become great among you must be your servant, and whoever wants to be first must be your slave—just as the Son of Man did not come to be served, but to serve, and to give his life as a ransom for many. (Matthew 20:25-28 NIV; see also Mark 10:42-45)

Read the Scripture carefully, however, and you'll note the complications in the passage. What are all the implications of becoming a servant? How often is *slave* associated with servant leadership? How would a leader exhibit slave-like behaviors when leading? Jesus gave his life "as a ransom for many"; are we willing to link our eventual physical death—becoming a literal ransom for our followers—to current discussions of servant leadership? Biblically, this is a fairly narrow concept, which has become embellished with extrabiblical meanings.

Paul's claim to be a "servant for Jesus' sake" and use of the term *co-worker* suggests the application of the servant leader model. But what does that mean for Paul? What do management experts (other than Jesus and Paul) say on this topic? Greenleaf himself described it as "a natural feeling that one wants to serve."

Then conscious choice brings one to aspire to lead. Such a person is sharply different from one who is a leader first, perhaps because of a need to assuage an unusual power drive or to acquire material possessions. The difference manifests itself in the care taken by the servant, first to make sure that other people's highest priority needs are being served. The test I like best, though difficult to administer, is: Do those served grow as persons; do they, while being served, become healthier, wiser, freer, more autonomous, more likely themselves to become servants? And, what is the effect on the least privileged person in society; will she or he benefit, or at least, not be further deprived? No one will knowingly be hurt, directly or indirectly.[17]

David Heenan, Craig Pearce and Jay Conger, and Jean Lipman-Blumen use terms like *co-leaders, shared leadership* and *connective leadership*; their research delves deeper into the complexities of this idea.[18] Max De Pree speaks of leading without power, which may be the real essence of leadership itself.[19] As mentioned above, if power is used, whether for good or evil, the behavior or activity may be something other than leadership. In fact, our own thinking as management professors is that leadership may best be considered a dimension of management (something Peter Drucker suggested) and, correspondingly, that leadership occurs when the power differential approaches zero. So if power is present, which in itself is not necessarily a bad thing, some sort of management is taking place because managers exercise power and authority—usually appropriately—in numerous ways.[20]

> At Corinth the toxic leaders were the "big-shot apostles" and the "pseudo-apostles." Obviously, Paul was not toxic, but in his attempts to deal with them he was clearly battered.
>
> Servant leadership has a place among Christ followers but only if it truly sets us apart as people who have the heart of Christ and are willing to serve as he served, recognizing the power of his words: "So you want first place? Then take the last place. Be the servant of all" (Mark 9:35).

Sometimes followers have a higher expectation for clear (or even forceful) direction than a leader does, which can confuse the leader in her attempts to be a servant. It can also cause a breakdown of communication and an abdication of responsibility for results where a leader attempts to be collaborative at all costs. Lack of direction, of managing, of *exercising* leadership, can just as quickly create chaos among these types of followers and allow silos (self-protecting units incapable of reciprocal operations) to fester. Perhaps we need to step back and realize that in one sense everyone in an organization *serves.* Support functions *serve* the mission as well as serving the operations functions; operational people *serve* the mission and the customer, and so on. And, of course, the leader serves everyone.

Peter Drucker says the manager is a servant. But he then clearly asserts that the manager serves the *institution*, and not its employees, customers or shareholders.

> His master is the institution he manages and his first responsibility must therefore be to it. His first task is to make the institution, whether business, hospital, school, or university, perform the function and make the contribution for the sake of which it exists.[21]

"Keep your eye on the task, not on yourself. The task matters, and you are a servant."[22] Servanthood must contribute to the institution's performance. If the institution or organization does not perform, it has no reason to exist (and servant leadership becomes irrelevant). Of course, the manager can generate performance through good leadership, ethical behaviors and affirming relationships with followers and subordinates; but the priorities must never be confused.

In the final analysis, for those who refuse to part with the term *servant leaders* (and especially if you think you are one), have someone check with your followers anonymously. Remember, no recriminations! The only true test for a so-called servant leader is a confidential reality check with the followers.

EXECUTIVE AND LEGISLATIVE LEADERSHIP

Big idea: *If you are approaching the legislative end of the leadership continuum, don't be surprised if you can't manage change or collapse in crisis.* We would assume that more executive forms of leadership would emerge in an emergency or a military situation where command and control would be preferred. Yet it is possible that an organization might drift the other direction, toward legislative leadership, as turbulence disintegrated into warring factions. The Corinthians would validate this—crisis can lead to rule by fragmented stakeholders and constituencies, resulting in toxic situations, broken systems and battered leaders. So wouldn't legislative leadership be a good thing? As long as the organization functions appropriately and effectively, a decentralized and dispersed organization could weather the storms—this is the strength of the franchise approach. But "a large number of institutions today employ governance structures inconsistent with their current activity."[23] Although legislative leadership is effective in the right context, organizations should function dynamically across this continuum. For example, at a time when they might benefit from some executive decision making, their organization may be too diffuse.

Diffuse decision making can be defined as follows:

- Several individuals are involved in decision making.

- These individuals are in different organizational levels, organizational units (at the same hierarchical level) or geographic locations.

- The decision is partitioned into several activities.

- Considerable time elapses between initiation and termination of the activity resulting in the decision (i.e., the point in time at which the decision is *made* is not distinct).

- A final decision results but is not rigid at any point in time (i.e., some flexibility continues to be exercised by participants in the decision).

Do these definitions sound familiar? We once worked on an ethnographic management study of an organization and began to understand its idiosyncrasies only when we finally saw an organization chart. It looked like a plate of spaghetti thrown against a wall. All five definitions above were represented in nearly every decision. Even the smallest decision could be co-opted by five to ten other people at different levels and in different locations around the world. It was an organization essentially condemned to constant crisis, without hope of innovation or change. Insiders thought everyone operated that way.

As appropriate as diffuse decision making and complex governance may be for an organization in stasis, change and crisis now rule almost everywhere. And if any place remains in stasis, we would all like to know who and where. (Nan Keohane allegedly said once that when doomsday came she wanted to be at Duke University, because everything there took a year longer; but not even Duke is in stasis.)

Experience would suggest that radical corrections in governance invariably happen too late. Try placing different organizations you know somewhere on this executive/legislative continuum. It should be clear to most that the academic community fits a model of legislative leadership and underscores the complexity of this management environment. In fact, true effectiveness appears sometimes to be possible only in a context of pure collaboration. Diffuse decision making connects faculties, the board, donors, sometimes a supervising denomination, local government, students and even nearby residents. A striking example of this is the multiyear odyssey that Westmont College in Santa Barbara, California, faced when attempting to expand facilities. The board and senior leaders juggled complicated stakeholder relationships until success was finally achieved.

Many churches might tend toward the other direction, especially if led by a charismatic senior pastor. Someone like Jim Jones can illustrate a worst-case scenario for executive leadership. Either extreme of the continuum can create problems.

> Even though Paul is essentially powerless at the beginning of 2 Corinthians, the crisis requires that he, with only God and his often-questioned apostolic authority to depend on, move the organization (at least temporarily) back toward the executive leadership model.

Old organizational aphorisms such as "authority must equal responsibility" fly to the winds. The senior executive of an institution managing complex governance and diffuse power structures is still responsible for the performance and results of the organization even if she does not possess the authority or power to make decisions alone. Yet when these organizations or communities fail to perform, it is not the board or faculty who are fired.

Complexity accelerates in turbulent times. Conventional emergency management organizations simply shift to executive leadership structures—effectively, military-like command and control—and manage the problem. Social sector organizations, unless their chief mission revolves around relief or crisis, face a more uncertain management challenge. Academic institutions confront added awkwardness due to the legislative leadership model; and, when the faith component of the academic faith community is manifested, the final layer of complexity is imposed. Charles Perrow's theories of complexity and coupling (described in chapter four), explain how academic organizations may be initially less vulnerable in turbulent times; but the trial of managing in the pure collaborative environment of legislative leadership, once the crisis begins, yet remains.

In the Corinthian case, a simple explanation of a shift toward legislative leadership by a group facing turmoil does not work. They created their own turmoil, beginning with irresponsible followership that allowed pseudo- or false apostles to exercise toxic leadership. The church became an organization thriving on discord and leadership apparently vacillating among Paul, some heavy-handed big-shot apostles, and quarreling factions.

In a less toxic setting, complex governance and diffuse decision making might have worked. As it turned out, Paul needed to impose strong executive leadership to bring a scattered group back to functionality.

A Final Thought: Am I a Toxic Leader?

Two reactions immediately result in every session when Professor Lipman-Blumen initially mentions the term *toxic leader*. First, every listener can think of one each has worked for. Second, every listener almost automatically shrugs off the possibility that the term may apply to him or her.

In the midst of enthusiastically cataloguing the various injustices that another leader may have perpetrated on others or us, we might need to work through our own "due diligence" and explore our personal capacity as leaders for battering followers. Without this honest appraisal we have no right to complain about those who batter us.

A while ago, Wesley was reflecting on toxic leadership with a class of senior executives. Jean Lipman-Blumen and Hal Leavitt (who wrote *Top Down: Why Hierarchies Are Here to Stay and How to Manage Them More Effectively*) had been class speakers, and the executives had read their books prior to the discussion. Over lunch four or five students paused, looked at each other, and said, "But *we're* toxic leaders!" We all agreed that each of us acted out aspects of toxicity in our day-to-day managerial lives. An only half-in-jest suggestion pointed toward some sort of twelve-step self-help program for toxic leaders.

That we could even admit our toxic tendencies spoke of the character of the executives in the room. We were all struck by our various actions and behaviors in our daily work life that hurt followers and us, as well as limit our organization's performance and results. Once aware of our problem, most of us will hopefully seek a solution, recognizing that self-regulation is part of our job as a leader. However many leaders still refuse to confront the signs of toxicity and instead assault their followers until they are stopped or retire.

It is easier to recall occasions when we have been bullied than it is to remember when we have done the bullying. Most complex are those situations where we firmly believe we acted appropriately and an overly sensitive follower misunderstood; toxic followers can manipulate a precarious situation to their own ends through an inappropriate response to a perfectly appropriate action by a leader. When trust is in short supply or gone altogether, the leader's attempts to define reality becomes more difficult for both leader and follower.

Just as a member of Alcoholics Anonymous begins the pilgrimage to sobriety by confessing, "I am an alcoholic," *all* leaders should start by recognizing their capacity for toxicity and begin working toward wholeness and eventually deeper effectiveness. The pride or fear in a manager that forestalls this process conveniently and temptingly transfers the onus and burden to the follower. A lack of courage underlies the inability of a leader to confess this flaw, but all leaders experience these shortcomings to various degrees.

On the other hand, followers can become toxic and create some fairly noxious issues in their own right. Eventually, this results in battered leaders. If there can be a patron saint of battered leaders it would be the apostle Paul.

TOOLBOX

Jean Lipman-Blumen is a formidable observer of toxic leadership and offers some of the best insights into their activities and destructive tendencies.

Toxic leaders leave their followers worse off than they found them, sometimes even eliminating—by undermining, firing, disenfranchising, imprisoning, incapacitating, torturing, or even killing—many of their own people.

They consciously feed their followers reassuring illusions that enhance their own power and impair the followers' capacity to act independently (e.g., by persuading followers that only the leader has the appropriate answers).

Toxic leaders subvert those structures and processes intended to generate truth and excellence. They undermine civil liberties and due process through authoritarian initiatives, including informally or formally stifling criticism and teaching followers (sometimes by intimidation and authoritarianism) to comply with the leader's directives.

They play to the followers' basest fears and needs, even

misleading them through deliberate misdiagnoses of problems. Sometimes, they treat their own followers well, but persuade them to hate and/or destroy others.

Some toxic leaders maliciously set their followers not only against outsiders, but also against one another. They maintain power through intimidation and terror and resort to scapegoating the weak and the despised.

At times, toxic leaders display their addiction to power by using improper means to cling to it.

They often weaken the legal processes for selecting and supporting new leaders.

They fail to nurture other leaders, including their own successors (with the occasional exception of blood kin), by building totalitarian or narrowly dynastic regimes.

At the lower end of toxicity, leaders ignore or promote incompetence and corruption. They fail to understand the nature of relevant problems and consistently perform ineffectively in leadership situations.

For a helpful exercise, take some version of 2 Corinthians from a website and paste it in a word-processing document. Set the right margin a few inches from the right edge of the page to create white space next to your text. Then read through, marking a TL for toxic leadership, L for positive leadership characteristics, F for follower characteristics, and TF for behaviors indicating toxic following. Jot any other thoughts that spring to mind as you re-read the book. Whatever Scripture version you use, look for words that describe leadership and management. This reinforces the strengths of 2 Corinthians as a leadership text and produces a list that might be compared to Lipman-Blumen's.

For example, using Today's New International Version (TNIV)

we note that the problem leader "has grieved all of you" (2:5). More generally, toxic leaders use "secret and shameful ways" and "deception," and "distort the word of God" (4:2). They put "stumbling blocks" in the paths of others (6:3), "command" them (8:8), and set up arguments and pretensions against the knowledge of God (10:5). The toxic leader preaches a different Jesus (11:4), in a different spirit proclaiming a different gospel, and presents himself as a super-apostle (11:5; 12:11).

The Corinthians, thanks to the misguided efforts of the leader who had "grieved" all of them, are clearly worse off. It appears that one of the Corinthian super-apostles worked with great energy to discredit Paul, persuading the Corinthians to think of him negatively. The net result created dissension within the group, as evidenced by the "stumbling blocks" Paul references. To keep power, these super-apostles preached a different Jesus.

Feeding illusions to our followers is deceptive, and many toxic leaders have used God's Word to do this. Certainly, the Word is a "structure intended to generate truth and excellence."[24] Distorting God's Word features prominently in the sordid history of toxic Christian leaders. Nearly every indicator of toxic leadership finds a home in the behaviors of the Corinthian super-apostles.

Yet Paul, in the midst of turmoil and rebellion, despite fractured relationships, toxic super-apostles and rabid follower behaviors, keeps his eye on the organization's performance. No leader could be clearer about the organization's outcomes. Read through 2 Corinthians and other letters, making a list of what Paul desires for the followers of Christ. This is how Paul understands the performance of his organization—the body of Christ in these local places.

These People Can't Be Led

A colleague in a different academic department inherited a hornet's nest of conflict. It was both perplexing and tragic. He lamented that "these people can't be led!"

How had the situation deteriorated to the point where this conclusion resulted? And why? Was there any hope?

In reading between the lines of the apostle Paul's management case study, perhaps we can sense his own regret in realizing that "these people can't be led." It may be, as social theorists would say, that Paul was no longer the prototypical leader the Corinthians wanted. Although he had initiated the church and advised, taught, loved and prayed for the group, over time the group came to represent something other than the original vision; either they had changed or Paul had changed.

The crux of this chapter is the exploration of particular follower issues that batter leaders. Followers show up increasingly in recent studies. Barbara Kellerman's *Followership* proposes six assumptions:

- *Followers constitute a group* that, although amorphous, nevertheless has members with interests in common.

- While followers by definition lack authority, at least in relation to their superiors, *they do not by definition lack power and influence.*

- Followers can be *agents of change.*

- Followers ought to support good leadership and *thwart bad leadership.*

- *Followers who do something are nearly always preferred* to followers who do nothing.

- Followers can create change by circumventing their leaders and joining with other followers instead.[1]

These aspects apply to a variety of followers and especially to the group in Corinth. Common interests and shared purpose originally united this group, but they appear to be unraveling somewhat. Part of Paul's task will be to refocus on these.

Followers clearly have power and influence. In the Corinthian situation turbulence is breaking out as followers flex their muscles. While never denying the importance of followers requiring the independence and authority to do their jobs, we posit that power can be a tricky proposition wherever and whenever it is wielded, including by followers. Change can clearly result from the actions of followers, just as the reluctance to act by followers can stall needed confrontation and change.

Kellerman's most dramatic example of followers leading is, of course, the resistance movement within the Holocaust that she explores in depth. Likewise, legitimate dissent is a prerequisite to real discussion of issues and informed decision making, managing change and adopting innovations in any organization. There are, however, circumstances where followers fail to *support good leadership or thwart bad leadership* (her point 4) but rather simply act in a contradictory manner, frequently without considering the impact of their misplaced loyalty and misguided behaviors.

Followership is the one factor that all definitions of leadership include. Leadership is a relationship, and like all relationships, it requires at least two parties: a leader and a follower. Both players are critical to the relationship. Both are necessary if leadership is to be exercised. Since leadership is primarily a relationship of influence, both parties have some influence, and unless someone chooses to accept the influence, no leadership has been exercised. By seeking to influence outcomes, followers provide some measure of leadership in particular situations. Followers also seek to influence outcomes.[2] In many ways leadership actually rests in the hands of followers. Leaders, then, are dependent on followers who choose to accept their influence.

There is and always should be an accountability between leader and led that holds to truth. If I am a bad or toxic leader, I should not be surprised if my behaviors are challenged. However, if I am leading congruently with the organization's values and mission, the responsible follower should give me the benefit of the doubt. This is why trust is so important. If guarded, it will buy the leader the time needed for being believed or vindicated when making an unpopular decision.

The Corinthians were deluded by new leadership and found it difficult to stay aligned with Paul. They also became enveloped in what Kellerman describes as *circumventing their leaders and joining with other followers* (her point 6). We will spend much of this chapter dealing with issues like mobbing and triangulation that result when followers gang up with other followers to circumvent their leaders and create organizational dysfunction as well as misery for the leader.

THE CORINTHIAN ORGANIZATION

In the case of the Corinthian church, Paul removes power from the equation by saying that they are partners, working together.

He has made the power differential zero by reframing the discussion and repositioning the dialogue.

> Now, are you ready for the real reason I didn't visit you in Corinth? As God is my witness, the only reason I didn't come was to spare you pain. I was being considerate of you, not indifferent, not manipulative.
>
> We're not in charge of how you live out the faith, looking over your shoulders, suspiciously critical. We're partners, working alongside you, joyfully expectant. I know that you stand by your own faith, not by ours. (2 Corinthians 1:23-24)

It is up to the Corinthians how they live, the choices they make, how they perceive the situation, and how they act on it. He is not looking over their shoulders—not willing to second-guess them. Phrases like "not suspiciously critical," "we're partners," "working alongside you" and "joyfully expectant" reinforce that in partnerships each is independent, equal standing on their own. Paul wants the Corinthians to see their relationship, at least at this point, as a flat one, not a hierarchy. He explains the reasons behind his actions by appealing to reason, asking them to be objective. Emphasizing the cognitive is not an effective approach. The phrase "stand by your own faith, not by ours" also recognizes that if they have problems they are of their own making—their own faith issues, not his.

The New Testament is filled with material that relates to organizations. Much of the more practical guidance it contains deals with relationships as well as with structure, accountability, roles, conflicts, and resolutions within organizations. So it should not be a surprise that the foundational follower issue in this case has broad organizational implications. But the text is not always clear. Different translations of the Corinthian case contribute to the confusion. For example, in 2 Corinthians 3:7 the TNIV uses "ministry" whereas *The Message* uses "government." The former can be perplexing, because English speakers will immediately think of the Christian "ministry," when the word is actually closer to "administration." *The Message* may thus be more accurate.

It is interesting that the Greek word διάκονος is where we get our word *deacons*. In the book of Acts, to relieve themselves of certain administrative tasks, the apostles appointed seven deacons. The term has created confusion since. Some have seen the term as a sign of servanthood. That may, however, be the equivalent of perceiving the secretary-general of the United Nations as the head typist in the UN's clerical pool. It is probably safer to understand, in general, these people serving in leadership capacities in some form of evolving organization.[3] Contextually, it is apparent that the lessons of the Corinthian case range far beyond church or "ministry" situations and, in fact, address many challenges across businesses, agencies, and social sector nonprofits.

Organizational Variations

In any management context, power differentials operate to varying extents. The appropriate authority delegated to a manager by a board and CEO, designed to equip the person to carry out assigned responsibilities, is a simple necessity. Other power may be given temporarily to a task force or committee. Following appropriate means, we allow our leader/manager to exercise this power in our organizational life together; even in the philosophical ideal of the flat organization, power thrives and gets used.

Whether flat or not, relationships in organizations tend toward complexity. Confusion between allies and confidants is one problematic area. An important distinction helps explain how leaders can misunderstand followers and contribute to problems.

Allies cross some organizational boundary to share your values or strategies. They are *not* loyal to you personally but to their own issues, projects or expectations. In coalitions, networks or other alliances they perform the useful service of providing a rational voice that transcends agenda.[4]

Confidants belong to you, can handle your deepest thoughts, are loyal and create a safe place for you to share your pain. Spouses and good friends often provide this service but may not necessarily be honest with you. In fact some of your closest supporters may find it especially difficult to tell you the truth because of the relationship: "It is not just that they don't want to hurt us. They want to believe."[5]

Allies are not the same as confidants! Do not mistake the two. Tasking an ally with the work of a confidant leads to difficulties.

Because he reported to a toxic leader who made everything personal, "Warren" began confiding in allies. His mastery at networking, tight grasp of strategy and consistent values in managing projects attracted supporters. As long as he stuck to the expectations of his alliance, things went well.

In leading his team, Warren sometimes reverted to a community agitator style, almost artificially creating crises with outsiders to stimulate the team to greater performance. Long-standing challenges of differentiating between his role as team leader and his own notions of self meant that role-generated conflict became personal. Warren misunderstood his network of allies and used it like a supportive group of confidants. The tensions of dealing with the toxic leader pushed Warren to muttering to people who had no personal loyalty to him. Quite naturally gossip spread, stirring up tensions and hard feelings, and Warren had to move on.

Followers are not automatically confidants. In fact, it is usually a bad idea to step out of a role of focusing followers around a purpose or crisis-driven effort just to share your angst. You should never assume that your team of followers will provide a safe place to vent. Their responsibility is to perform and to be effective at their tasks, not to salve your wounds. This requires a sort of detachment that may be difficult in relational communities. The military's requirement of a formal distance between officers and enlisted ranks is not always easy or sensitively handled in other types of organizations.

The apostle Paul's relationships with leaders, followers and colleagues range across the spectrum. It is not always clear whether others around him understand when they are allies and when they are confidants. He knocks heads with the elders in Jerusalem, gets kicked around by various followers around the Mediterranean Basin, and has good and bad days with traveling companions and colleagues.

Paul seems to struggle with certain relationships, in part, due to his sometimes cantankerous personality and also because of misalignment between what an individual wants from him and what he is able or willing to give, based on what he understands God has called him to be and do. At times he appears to cross boundaries.

Paul writes of deeply passionate friendships and the painful wounds they create. Driven by a great love for his Master and for others, his organizational perceptions and responses are varied and paradoxical at times. But it is clear Paul faced a Corinthian gang so toxic that strong words, impassioned pleading and significant threats were often called for. The organization at Corinth clearly had constituencies. The challenge is determining at what point they turned into mobs, intent on bludgeoning a leader.

A PALACE COUP

Experienced followers can exercise power quite competently and often appropriately. But what happens when both leader and organization collapse as followers assert an inappropriate role? When does adhocracy become "toxhocracy"? Where is the line crossed from participatory decision making to mob rule? Whenever it is crossed, beat-up leaders are often the victims and failed organizations often follow.

A classic follower response in certain situations is the palace coup. This is the point when the mutiny begins flexing destructive muscles, and everyone but the leader realizes a corner has been turned. We all know of situations where a powerful and evil despot abused followers, whether in nation-states or in organizations. We are less convinced that simply misguided, or even evil, followers can bring down an otherwise competent leader on their own. However, there should not always be a presumption of innocence when confronting followers who have an agenda, as they can eventually destroy leaders and organizations.

The hornet's nest situation Warren faced resulted from preexisting cliques, the removal of a fomenting former executive who then remained within the organization, ambivalent leadership further up the food chain, and continuing irresolution. The entrenched toxic clique perceived that lack of directive leadership higher in the hierarchy permitted their ongoing behaviors.

Two are considerably more powerful than one. *One annoying follower may be pesky, but two annoying followers can create a conspiracy.* In the histories of the navies of the world, significant mutinies have resulted from the collusion of two malcontents. Married couples in organizations can often be perceived as automatic conspiracies, whether they agree on anything or not. Academic couples in universities and churches perplex colleagues, followers and superiors when their perceived influence is greater than the sum of the parts.

Three annoying followers can launch a mob. From this point on, toxic followers can reach supercritical mass and replicate exponentially. Social identity theory, which looks at group processes and intergroup relations, can help us understand this dynamic. (See more on this in chapter eight.) The leader of a group has the power to define what the group stands for and the social identity of its members; but in turn, the leader's identity, as a construction of group processes, is dependent on the nature and standards of the group. Once a significant number or influential body within the group questions the legitimacy of the leader, the leader's days may be numbered.

There is no perfect organization, not even the church, and there are no perfect leaders. So dissension and muttering will always exist; the issue is its potential for disrupting groups. For managers and leaders, it simply goes with the turf—no group of followers exists where conflict is not naturally present. Conspiracies will wither on the vine if conflict is managed.

> Paul seeks to give followers freedom to develop as leaders in their own context and yet to steer the organization so that it doesn't collapse while those emerging leaders develop. This is especially difficult if the leader is operating as a virtual influence from a distance, as Paul is regarding Corinth.

GROUPTHINK

Related to the conspiracy is the phenomenon of "groupthink,"[6] where group norms become more powerful than critical thinking. Group direction and momentum are maintained despite bad results and individually troubled consciences:

> The more amiability and esprit de corps there is among the members of a policy making in-group, the greater the danger that independent critical thinking will be replaced by groupthink, which is likely to result in irrational and dehumanizing actions directed against out groups.[7]

A herd finds independent thinking a challenge. It takes courage for a follower to take on other members of a group if the follower depends on this group for friendship, affirmation, support or validation of any kind. A clear opportunity cost decision will be made by the follower at any point where the loss of these might be imagined. There is a high price to be paid for going against the group.

But hopefully groupthink will not survive strong and appropriate leadership.

In many settings individuals without formal power can still exercise leadership. Power and influence can be wielded by followers, and followers who exercise leadership can greatly benefit organizations.

The dependency on followers for leadership is what makes the relationship so important. Referred to as *adaptive* action by Ronald Heifetz, leader-follower interaction involves a process that requires leaders and followers to adapt to circumstances and, particularly, to facilitate positive change in organizations. In a later chapter we will talk about how a subordinate informally leading without power can be a good thing.

Constituencies

In this study *constituency* means any subgroup guided by a single, focused agenda formed against the background of an organization's operations. This is a management perspective that identifies follower behaviors as they coalesce around an issue and is very different from a political constituency, which identifies a group of stakeholders served by an elected official.

A constituency within an organization may aggregate around a problem, an opportunity or a completely random perception. It is characterized by activities that may not necessarily be in the best interest of the organization but can take on lives of their own (or a *meme*, as described earlier). The constituency lobbies, legislates, importunes and urges for a cause that is uniquely its own. Essentially, it does not exist except in some kind of opposition—at some degree of intensity—to the primary direction or mission of the host organization. Constituencies may not be all bad—some whistleblower movements begin this way. But they can create problems for the manager or executive because they diverge from the mission—an appropriate direction in which the organization is heading. The constituency places its needs and entitlements ahead of the organization's.

Membership in a constituency may shift or be temporary, but often it congregates around a strong personality. An informal leader within an organization can gain power and a platform by emphasizing a negative perception or criticizing an initiative or a legitimate leader. A constituency is capable of easily circumventing the direction of a legitimate leader.

Blaming

"Culture of blame" is becoming a common organizational cliché. Extending its meaning by connecting the concept to biology—

and the more colorful image of a "culture" grown in a laboratory—might be fitting. In the petri dish of a dysfunctional organization, blaming cultures can be noxious, pungent and toxic.

Constituencies sometimes use this tool, which creates silos and other aberrations, and damages the effectiveness of organizations. Personal and workgroup preservation become more important than the organizational mission. Created and nurtured by fear, negative behaviors quash risk taking and subvert accountability by excessive reliance on form over substance. Fear further forms alternative realities, documented in mounds of paper, and pursued by rabid adherence to policies, procedures and rules. The ensuing bureaucracies are organizational coping mechanisms at best, but can suck the life out of individuals and teams in much the same way that even large animals can be sucked into quicksand. (See *system fatigue syndrome* in chapter four.)

We are all familiar with the way that many administrations, political and otherwise, blame the previous one for their problems. Issues that deal moral blows to us particularly require someone to blame. We recognize, as well, that we tend to take personal responsibility for successes but attribute blame to others for failures of which we are a part. But in many work situations blaming starts with small details. These are not really significant but over time create a climate of negativity.

For example, someone erroneously gets credit for the success of a project. Others who should have received credit may think the boss or team leader to be responsible for the slight. A climate of blame starts, building increasingly negative behaviors. Studies show that blame is contagious, spreads like wildfire and is amplified by insecurity.[8]

To atone for their sins on Yom Kippur the ancient Israelites would select an animal—a "scapegoat"—and push it out of town into the desert (see Leviticus 16). Obviously, the goat did nothing to deserve this, but it settled the corporate conscience of community members as well as meeting the requirements of the earlier covenant. In contemporary occurrence, the scapegoat, or "fall guy," serves to distract attention from real causes. This organizational behavior makes problematic issues superficial, artificially defusing and neutralizing a necessary reality. Blaming and scapegoating become embedded in cultural frames within organizations as alternatives to complex analysis and real change.

It is easiest to make the scapegoat the individual who is slightly different either in dress or behavior—that individual becomes a natural target. We see how Paul easily fit this paradigm when he began challenging the Corinthians for needing a leader who met their mental image of success, including financial success, cosmopolitan suavity and oratorical gifts.

Fundamentally, blame grows in organizational cultures where mistakes are not allowed. Punishment, criticism, or other forms of payback quash risk taking and neutralize innovation and creativity. Mary Pearson describes the characteristics of a blaming culture.

> There is an element of denial, hand in hand with a zealous can-do attitude. The chief executive officer may only want to hear about successes and become distressed when news of problems arises.
>
> In some cases, a boss who blows up over issues can keep underlings mortified about letting bad news filter up.
>
> There is no tolerance for mistakes, however minor, and those who make them are reprimanded or shamed in some way.

In a blaming culture, there is scant positive feedback for the things that go well, but there is swift negative feedback for the smallest of errors.

There are no rewards or recognition for taking calculated risks; therefore, most employees shy away from more challenging, high-risk issues, minimizing their exposure to fallout.

There's a lack of courage among middle managers for standing up for decisions, opinions, mistakes, and defending staff. Staff know this and feel vulnerable.

The paper trail is enormous. Several people or units sign off on every decision in order to spread the responsibility as thinly as possible.

No one wants to be on the hook. This can manifest itself in too many committees, excessive bureaucracy and confusing organization structures.

Usually the scapegoat is someone at or near the bottom of the hierarchy, as more powerful players become quite adept at avoiding blame themselves.[9]

MONEY

Second Corinthians has much to say about the confusion surrounding the use and abuse of financial resources. The money thread surfaces repeatedly in Paul's remonstrations and captures our attention merely by how many times it is mentioned.

Most of us are weary of the frequent and sordid tales of nonprofit and religious organizations (or their leaders) squandering the faithful gifts of small donors on travel, yachts and bling, but with relief we note that Paul holds and defends precisely the opposite position. He doesn't want money from the Corinthians;

in fact, he wants to be identified as someone who does not require the resources of others. His response is paradoxical, counterintuitive and utterly appropriate.

Toxic followers, however, attempt to use money to lure Paul into a culture of greed, apparently widely understood around the Mediterranean Basin as a Corinthian peccadillo. Timothy B. Savage's description of Corinth evokes a Wild West boomtown, featuring brash entrepreneurs flaunting new wealth and conspicuous consumption as the norm—maybe a little like Silicon Valley in the 1990s.[10] Wesley worked with the Ukrainian government in crisis management after the demise of the Soviet Union, and in the heady days that followed in rowdy Kiev, the new "business stars" could quickly be spotted— any new American sports utility vehicle (SUV) on the street contained at least one. We can imagine Corinth being similar to Kiev in that era.

A testosterone-charged business culture, where bald ambition and shameless self-promotion predicates the corporate "best practices" metric, surely clashed resoundingly with the values Paul promoted that were aimed at "demolishing that entire massively corrupt culture" (2 Corinthians 10:4-5). The boasting he opposed in chapter 10, according to Savage, might better be translated "godless self-commendation."[11]

The love of money and associating wealth with personal goodness or identity can corrupt and stain when it captures a community or organization. The resulting confusion—as individuals view poverty as a sign of individual lapses or equate spirituality with prosperity—will fog previously clear norms and expectations. Wealth inequities, depending on how they are treated, can be even more poisonous.

TRIANGULATION

Little doubt exists that Paul, exercising apostolic authority, established the Corinthian church and led them, whether in the flesh or from afar, through letters. When the super-apostles stepped into the triangle after the misguided, manipulative, and toxic Corinthian followers invited the super-apostles into the mix, the new dynamic neutralized an appropriate relationship, negated Paul's authority and validated a new toxic leadership.

Toxic leaders at Corinth formed the third point of a triangle, creating a situation that marginalized Paul and allowed the Corinthians to bypass him.

Once, Wesley had a boss a level or two above him ("Don") whom he respected very much. In a moment of weakness—not managing social awareness very well that day—Wesley let slip a slightly critical comment about his own direct supervisor ("Fred"). Don immediately replied, "I won't have this conversation without Fred in the room." Wesley realized at once that Don possessed robust built-in defenses against triangulation. He refused to marginalize Fred by allowing words to be spoken behind his back. Wesley's triangle attempt collapsed in a heap, and he learned a valuable lesson.

Paul's original followers were denying his right to speak into their lives; he was in a triangle that resisted his leadership.[12] When Wesley made his minor attempt to exclude Fred, Don's response could have sealed it with a nod of agreement or confirmation of his assessment had he had less character or organizational savvy. That is all it takes to build a triangle.

What happens when your boss gives your followers or subordinates permission to ignore you? Dysfunction erupts when a thriving triangle slips the surly bonds and launches into full flight. Your followers effectively just denied you your right to tell them what to do by inappropriately (or even covertly) inviting your boss into the mix, especially if that boss is not supporting you. The boss can then take advantage of the disappointment, disaffection or other negative emotion to pursue a path to diminish your power without confronting the situation directly and thus avoid blame for the outcome.

Kate Ludeman and Eddie Erlandson describe an "alpha triangle," in which a leader is identified as a villain by followers who are victims and the leader's boss jumps into the fray as hero to rescue the victims.[13] In an alpha triangle, all have a stake in perpetuating the dysfunction because each role gives satisfaction arising from the personality types linked to the roles. Unlike the triangle Paul found himself in, there are no innocents in an alpha triangle.

In Paul's case we can define *toxic triangles* where the leader in the middle is essentially blameless, and hero and victims gang up to ambush their quarry. This can start as a toxic triangle but flares up into full-blown mobbing in certain settings when the proper conditions are met.

A third form of triangulation blooms in the fertile

> The super-apostles vying for power and position joined forces with the toxic followers at Corinth. They evolved into a mob and became a critical mass opposing Paul's rightful leadership.
>
> It is likely that the super-apostles never faced the full, face-to-face fury of a righteously indignant Paul. At least we cannot find references to this in the received texts, so some seem to think he actually appeared weaker when he showed up in person.

ground of failed bullying. It can emerge as a follow-up strategy when the bully fails in his initial approach against a particular target. Aware of the existence of aggrieved followers, the bully rides to the rescue. Although bullies by definition lack courage and steer away from open conflict, they can ride the coattails of others' unhappiness to emerge as the appreciated hero, even as a mid-level manager.

On the other hand, where a competent leader speaks truth to power, a bully can end up exposed and embarrassed. Where a leader manages the process strategically, the same individual can be defused. At the same time, a leader rightly resisting a bullying boss can inadvertently channel toxic followers to creative anarchy. The corresponding toxic ambivalence on the part of the bullying boss creates warm, dark places where mobs form. It is a form of tacit approval, and toxic followers can be quick to catch on.

Mobs can form without triangulation, but they won't survive long where good leaders spot them and shut down their momentum. Truly devastating mobs need triangles for sustainability.

MOBBING

Paul finds himself mobbed both physically, in the riots and tumults that he often describes, and psychically, in the ganging-up behaviors exhibited by his fellow believers in Corinth. The latter type of mobbing is quite effective in battering leaders.

As an area of inquiry, mobbing is relatively new. Heinz Leymann is regarded as the field's pioneer, and resources are growing across the web, identifying cases and generating analysis. Most recent thinking deals with workplace hostility and bullying, but the findings are distinctive in identifying the ganging-up component, using rumor and innuendo. "Status-blind harassment"[14] can happen to anyone (not just those in protected classes). Mobbing involves hostile and unethical communication conducted in a systematic manner by one or more individuals primarily toward one individual, who is then forced into a helpless and defenseless role and held there by ongoing activities. These actions occur on a frequent basis (at least once a week) over a long period of time (at least six months' duration). Because of the high frequency and long duration, this maltreatment results in considerable mental, emotional and social strain and is linked with post-traumatic stress disorder.[15]

Mobbing and bullying have clear distinctives. Bullying is more associated with leaders; mobbing finds its home more naturally among followers (see table 3.1). In the workplace, "an impassioned, collective campaign by colleagues to exclude, punish and humiliate a targeted worker" forms one definition of mobbing. "Conflict through which one individual is targeted by a group of colleagues on a *regular basis* over *several months* leaving the person in an *almost powerless* position" may be more precise. The three key factors are *ongoing activity* of *long duration* resulting in *diminished power*. Power in this context may simply mean an individual's ability to affect her environment or to accomplish the simplest tasks in a workday. Many of the examples address horizontal mobbing activity, essentially peer-driven, and often where leaders have no inkling that a subordinate is a target until the victim departs or sues. When superiors (who are sometimes thwarted bullies) join the mob, the victim may have no choice but to move on.[16]

Table 3.1. Bultena and Whatcott Differentiate Between Mobbing and Bullying *(See www .mobbing-usa.com/.) Like any theory these differences should be examined critically. Our study would suggest that these behaviors may occur wherever dysfunction is found.*

	BULLYING	MOBBING
Sector	Often public organizations (sales)	Often private organizations (higher education)
Harasser(s)	Single person (often a supervisor)	Colleagues
Target(s)	Weak or submissive	Above average performer
Motivation	Bully's motivation to achieve power	Threatened by victim's perceived power
Actions Derive from	Self-aggrandizement	Envy or jealousy
Triggering Situation	Bully's feelings of inadequacy	Organizational conflict
Desired Effects	Achieve a patsy	Drive out of organization
Methods	Elementary	Complex
Harassment Activities	Obvious abnormal interactions	Disguised as normal interactions
Attack	Direct	Indirect
Defense	Likely informal	Likely informal
Frequency	Single or regular occurrence, no specified pattern	Regular occurrence, at least once a week
Duration	Various durations	Long durations, at least for six months
When Victim Subsides	Victim loses effectiveness	Victim leaves organization
When Victim Resists	Bullies back off	Mobbers gather strength
Management	Often aligns with victim	Often aligns with mobbers
Harasser(s) Consequences	Often punished	Often unpunished
Victim Consequences	Loss of confidence and self-assurance, anger, illness, frustration, unemployment, doubts of sanity, stress	
Organizational Consequences	Turnover, decreased productivity, loss of effectiveness, creativity, reputation, commitment and key people	
Social Consequences	Unemployment, disaffection, court involvement	

Mobbing is indicated in the following:

- By standard criteria of job performance, the target is at least average, probably above average.

- Rumors and gossip circulate about the target's misdeeds: "Did you hear what she did last week?"

- The target is not invited to meetings or voted onto committees, is excluded or excludes herself.

- There is a collective focus on a critical incident that "shows what kind of man he really is."

- There is a shared conviction that the target needs some kind of formal punishment, "to be taught a lesson."

- The decision to punish is made with unusual timing, e.g., apart from the annual performance review.

- Emotion-laden, defamatory rhetoric about the target is found in oral and written communications.

- Formal expressions of collective negative sentiment are made toward the target, e.g. a vote of censure, signatures on a petition, meetings to discuss what to do about the target.

- The mobbers place a high value on secrecy, confidentiality and collegial solidarity.

- Diversity of argument is lost, so that it becomes dangerous to "speak up for" or defend the target.

- The target's real or imagined venial sins are added up to make a mortal sin that cries for action.

- The target is seen as personally abhorrent, with no redeeming qualities; stigmatizing, exclusionary labels are applied.

- Established procedures are disregarded, as mobbers take matters into their own hands.

- Independent, outside review of sanctions imposed on the target is resisted by the mobbers.

- Any appeals for outside help the target may make are met with outrage.

Mobbers fear violence from the target, or the target fears violence from the mobbers, or both.[17]

Peers and followers can excel at mobbing. Followers mobbing a leader, instead of the more typical horizontal behaviors, create unique scenarios. Sometimes there may be shadows of difference between abused followers resisting a toxic leader and toxic followers "wearing out" a battered leader. Exploring self-awareness is definitely called for.

The super-apostles and Corinthian followers had done this to Paul. Possibly some of the effectiveness in Paul's response to the Corinthians may lie in his refusal to take the abuse. He vigorously challenged the Corinthian assertion that he could not speak into the relationship. Even though the super-apostles presumed they were higher management, Paul shut down the problem by calling on what he considered the "highest" management—God.

Who are the more typical targets of mobbing? The authors of *The Starfish and the Spider* see change agents as likely mobbing victims.[18] It appears that targets are also former prototypical leaders who no longer exemplify the normative behavior of the group or organization.

A former faculty member at a prominent seminary describes her own case study as a victim of mobbing.[19] While there are a host of issues tucked inside her story, she makes the intriguing suggestion that a change in organizational governance was a contributing factor. She raises the question whether a move from shared-faculty decision making to more focused administrator-based decision making plays a role.[20]

It is undeniable that leadership plays a part—for better or worse—in mobbing. It will always be a leadership issue, whether we are victim, rescuer or perpetrator.

Barbara Kellerman describes the story of Peter Post, a vice president for marketing at Pfizer.[21] Post's followers apparently made the decision to stop reporting to him after Post made some sort of public criticism. Next his superiors stopped communicating, his secretary left, his office was moved to the hinterlands of the company, his email address stopped working, and his company cell phone was disconnected. Not surprisingly the story ends with his firing.

If not already present, triangulation can accelerate mobbing. The triangle is created by adding one or more power figures (supervisor, boss, consultant or others with some authority) to the mobbers who gang up on the leader, with implicit permission having been given. "Many of the victims are managers and supervisors, attacked or undermined by unscrupulous subordinates or peers—often with approval by higher management."[22]

It is interesting that according to Bultena and Whatcott, mobs take on above-average performers, perhaps even out of resentment or insecurity. Several of the mobbing scenarios we studied feature a clueless leader doing a competent job; the gathering storm of mobbers invariably surprises the person.

It appears that bullying might be more controllable in organizations than mobbing, which seems credible, unless the bully wields unique power or there is no place of appeal against the errant, mobbing behavior taking place within the organization.

TURNAROUNDS

Rescuing is a response loaded with complexities. On the one hand, every turnaround situation is essentially a rescue. Many CEOs generate well-deserved acclaim and exalted reputations by turning around faltering organizations. Business executives are well compensated if they become good at this. Boards aware of progressive or imminent decline in the corporation or nonprofit they govern look for a turnaround executive when deterioration or falling profitability threatens. Organizational rescuers often come from the outside. Senior leaders may imagine that an unknown or fresh face will have better results; alternatively, insiders who also know the quirks of the organization may be too smart to take on the challenge.

In addition, every organization and effective executive wants to invest in individuals who have potential but struggle with ignorance, self-sabotage, low skills, or lack social and emotional competencies. Leaders typically see this investment as staff development! Underlying it is an often passionate desire to fix people and coach them to new contributions. It means managing systems and people so that staff exercise responsibility for individual and group achievement and bring transformation and innovation.

This is a good thing. But the complexities inherent in human personalities and organizational cultures can generate unintended consequences. People especially can react if they sense they are being wrongly singled out or unfairly compared to high performers. The perception may be that "it is not my problem." What if I don't think I'm actually broken? Or what if I like where I am? Why rock the boat?

There also exist individual rescuers, those who try to save people by taking them on in jobs they can rarely be successful at.

They insist on regularly helping individuals who commit self-sabotage, shoot themselves in the foot, commit other job-endangering activities or generally do not perform. These individuals can be senior managers who always have one more "charity case" whom they protect for various reasons. It is important to make the distinction between staff development, or coaching to new levels of competence, and its toxic relative—rescuing.

Complacency in organizations breeds comfortable new cultural frames where many employees find happy homes for long careers. Clashes are certain in these days of change management when the comfortable inside meets the meaningful outside. Change is inevitable, but in dysfunctional places the intrigues associated with change are also inevitable. A turnaround specialist CEO will face challenges defining new realities in these places.

Most people do not really like change. If a bar is being raised, those challenged may gang up, opposing the manager by forming a constituency around a negative cause. A constituency burrowing underground or festering in an organization becomes a mob if not checked in time. We have come across several narratives where a senior leader may bring in a turnaround/rescue specialist for a department. Some new expectation has been set, and the imported manager is initially celebrated as the go-to fix-it person. In several of these cases the CEO, aware of the internal political implications of change, starts the process with a sense of latent or even unrecognized ambivalence that may only emerge when the natural turbulence of change bubbles to the surface. Mobs form when this senior leader's reluctance to lead, or to lead in new or socially non-normative ways, is introduced. This elicits a frenzy, which prompts a CEO, already familiar with the organization's quirks, belatedly to count the cost and sacrifice the imported manager, hoping that a more opportune moment for introducing change will come later.

Once again, a deadly triangle traps the imported manager who is only attempting to carry out the task she was hired to do. This may explain why catalysts usually last less than two years and can frequently become the scapegoat.

In one case, a manager was brought in to "bring the organization to a new level." The CEO believed in the cause, but the executive directly managing the imported manager found her threatening. The department managed by the imported person did not want the challenges of upping the quality of their work. The combination of an aloof CEO, a managing executive with personal agendas and an imported rescuer enabled a pack of circling sharks in the department, who then fed on the hapless manager. The rescuer was ridden out on a rail, very nearly tarred and feathered as well. Hope might have triumphed had the CEO exercised leadership over the triangle, but for various reasons this did not happen. Toxic ambivalence won the day.

The organizational lifespan of rescuers is problematic. If you are a turnaround rescuer type, take stock of the very real possibility that you will be sacrificed on the altar of exigency, often by means of triangles.

A Final Thought

It appears to be clear by this point in our study that we leaders are just as capable of battering others as we are of being battered ourselves, and also that the opportunities are numerous for being battered from above as well as from below. The next chapter explores a third and potentially more nettlesome area—the possibilities of being beaten up by the system itself. Leaders find this troubling because a faceless system is an intangible, and the factors contributing to it are difficult to identify as well as to correct. The solutions, therefore, are also more complex in application.

TOOLBOX

What kind of follower are you? Fill out the list in table 3.2.

Table 3.2. What Kind of Follower Am I?

ROLES		
disciple	*following*	Jesus
citizen	*following*	state
employee	*following*	supervisor
worshiper	*following*	deity
student	*following*	teacher
servant	*following*	master
partner	*following*	partner
manager	*following*	mission
postulant	*following*	vocation/calling
sheep	*following*	shepherd
decision maker	*following*	conscience
apprentice	*following*	master
	following	
	following	
	following	
	following	
	following	
	following	
	following	
	following	

Following is always about relationships. In table 3.3, list qualities and factors in being a good follower in column one; in column two list the opposite qualities and factors, which are characteristic of toxic followers.

Table 3.3. FOLLOWING Is Always About Relationships

Qualities of a Good Follower		Qualities of a Toxic Follower
trusting	vs	
humble	vs	
not triangulating	vs	
taking responsibility	vs	
eschewing conflict	vs	
reflecting brightness of another	vs	
	vs	
	vs	
	vs	
	vs	
	vs	
	vs	
	vs	

What kind of follower should you be? In the space below, draft a *credo*—an aspirational statement of what kind of follower you would like to be.

Groupthink is close to critical mass in Corinth. What characteristics of this group have led to their present situation?

Paul clearly saw rescuing in his mission to the Corinthian organization. What were the conditions present in his rescue operation?

> "Unless you integrate the vision of all constituencies into the long-range goal, you will soon lose support, lose credibility, and lose respect. After I'd been beaten to a pulp, I began to look at nonprofit executives who did successfully what I had unsuccessfully tried to do. I soon learned that they start out by defining the fundamental change that the nonprofit institution wants to make in society and in human beings; then they project that goal onto the concerns of each of the institution's constituencies."
>
> Peter Drucker, Managing the Nonprofit Organization

4

System Fatigue Syndrome

Sometimes **battering situations** simply don't make sense. When we have exhaustively catalogued every possibility, from bullies to mobbing and beyond, and we still can't understand the background for the assault, something more amorphous and indefinable may remain. In these cases, the deeper cultures, mythologies, sublimated corporate memory or other imponderables can help explain the backdrop for a battered leader. When the apostle Paul speaks of the "massively corrupt culture" (2 Corinthians 10:3-6), he is alluding to a system at work that is bigger and more powerful than the sum of the individual actors in it.

As Douglas McGregor—who identified Theory X and Theory Y in terms of how people perceive individuals within organizations—noted decades ago, assumptions about human nature become the basis of management and control systems that perpetuate themselves as we employees eventually come to behave according to the underlying assumptions that inform the way we are treated. The result is an organizational culture where the management and control systems reflect the character of the creators—how they act and what they reward, not what they say. At times, this means there may even be inherent and intrinsic evil in a failed community.[1] For want of a better term, we will name this "the system" and attempt to understand how it functions.

Systems are defined essentially as interacting components in organizational behaviors and structures. When the system is at fault we can develop system fatigue syndrome (SFS), where responsibilities are ignored or not assigned, solutions are unclear, inexplicable notions of turf block access to dialogue or reason, shared yet largely invisible cultural norms dominate (sometimes invisible because they may be ethically or morally inappropriate), or subtle informal power structures overwhelm the formal. These as well as other similar behaviors contribute to this organizational pathology.

Battering that is carried out by those above, who are responsible for leading us or those below, who are responsible for following us, shows up on our screen quite clearly. As we become aware of being beaten up by either bosses or followers, the source of the problem is visible; the toxic leaders and problematic followers have names, and eventually we can see actions and situations indicating when a situation first began to unravel.

But this third and final source of wear and tear on leaders is more perplexing and subtle. When the system is the culprit, it is harder to define the problem. Where ambiguity or complex layers and dimensions confound us, solutions to feeling knocked around come more slowly. We find it difficult to label the problem. Even when an individual can be linked to the issue, we discover that other complexities cloud how we sort out the fix. Something imponderable like "We have always done it this way" or "Policy prohibits that" pops up, and possible solutions drift away. The people involved are not solely responsible for the problem creating the pain. There are deeper forces at work.

System fatigue syndrome effectively kills innovation, drives away creativity and wearies good people out of the organization. Every leader hits this wall somewhere, and it is present in every organization that has existed for more than a few months. The impact ranges from momentarily annoying to deeply demonic—for anyone who has ever sincerely read the Bible the existence of principalities and powers is difficult to deny.

GENERAL SYSTEMANTICS

John Gall humorously labels system issues with tongue-in-cheek terms in his now-out-of-print *General Systemantics*.[2] Masking the pain we all feel as victims of systems with wry humor, Gall comes dangerously close to truth in his organizational subtleties. Take his Primal Scenario or Basic Datum of Experience: *Systems in general work poorly or not at all.* This is a creative start and sets aside the rose-colored glasses at the outset.

We raise questions about the systems approach to life since it is obvious that all types of institutions can get carried away with them, seeing systems or elaborate processes as the solutions to everything, when in fact they fail us regularly. Major disasters—such as Bhopal, India, where thousands of people were killed or injured due to a mechanical breakdown that was exacerbated by the failure of the human system, or airline nightmares where travelers are stuck on planes for hours without their basic

> *Consider the first-century communications challenges Paul faced, coupled with the various reports he was receiving on what was actually happening in Corinth over the time span of his two letters. Add to this travel time, varying levels of trust with the key players, the super-apostle shenanigans and the numerous other agendas percolating away, and you have a malfunctioning complex system probably approaching total nonfunctioning.*

human needs being met (which has led to changes in the law), or the 2010 Gulf of Mexico oil spill in which British Petroleum (BP) failed to understand the magnitude of the problem and thus its solutions were ineffective—all demonstrate aspects of the systems dilemma.

Sometimes smaller, but still as toxic, are instances where short-term corporate profit becomes the single driving force of a business or where founders, out of touch with current realities, continue traditional but outmoded practices in non-profit organizations, prompting highly qualified individuals to jump ship and younger, talented workers to bypass the organization. An overarching strategy like Six Sigma, a business management tool for improving quality, can become such a system; while it has its place and can be effective at improving quality in a variety of industries, once decision makers buy in, it becomes the unspoken, institutional solution to all barriers to growth or productivity.

How many times have we faced yet another new system proposal touted uncritically to solve a particular issue? Starting with the sensible assumption that it probably will not work sets the stage for a healthy skepticism. When organizations confound us, we may want to consider another of Gall's descriptors: "Complicated systems produce unexpected outcomes/the total behavior of large systems cannot be predicted."

We generally suppose that systems involve technology like circuit boards, mechanical devices and software, but this is not always the case. Many complex activities involving people in organizations have underlying systems and systemic explanations, forces that may or may not be clear to all involved. With such complexity comes unpredictability. Even in a highly technical context like BP's Gulf oil spill, some human being failed to arm the siren that would have signaled a problem (among other things), and serious consequences ensued.

According to Gall's Functional Indeterminacy Theorem, "In complex systems, malfunction and even total nonfunction may not be detectable for long periods, if ever." Perhaps best of all is Gall's Fundamental Law of Administrative Workings (F.L.A.W.): "Things are what they are reported to be. The real world is whatever is reported to the system." In other words, if it isn't official, it didn't happen. Add the corollaries to F.L.A.W.: "A system is no better than its sensory organs. To those within a system, the outside reality tends to pale and disappear."

In a later section on communities of systematic self-delusion in chapter five, we attempt to describe how the outside reality tends to pale and disappear for groups adrift.

Earlier we mentioned Max De Pree's dictum that the first task of a leader is "to define reality." In the context of F.L.A.W., his advice takes on new urgency. In addition, it is important to restate the obvious—that some aspects of trying to figure out organizations go beyond simple, analytical observations and methods and are beyond the reach of normal human interactions.

IMPONDERABLE COMPLEXITIES

Have you ever faced an organization that seems to take on a life of its own? Every thoughtful attempt fails, whether to form an objective assessment of its workings or to create a rational prediction of where it will go next. It is similar to trying to fit a water balloon into a box. When you push on one part, another part pops up in a different direction.

Some of this imponderable complexity can be explained by unseen powers that work behind and beneath the fabric of organizations we inhabit. For those who espouse biblically centered values and principles, it is unacceptable to deny these extra dimensions of spiritual activity, whether God-supporting or God-opposing. Throughout the rest of the New Testament and extensively in the Old Testament, these references surface in various forms. Paul persistently identifies the truth of opposition in spiritual realms to the faithful operation of the community in Corinth.

Others coming from very different religious positions often offer the same insights. Feng shui—an ancient Chinese system of aligning objects according to favorable force fields—as well as deeply rooted religious concepts opposing the worship of anyone or anything other than the one true God can create similar implications for organizations.

THE PAIN CONTINUUM

The pain Paul experienced in the Corinth case because of personal relationships is real, but not all the leadership problems he confronts can be blamed on toxic leaders or followers. In 2 Corinthians 2:9-11 Satan's "mischief" is one of many allusions to nonhuman powers at work in the group at Corinth. Time and distance compound Paul's attempts to stay on top of situations there. His clear sense of frustration in his correspondence recognizes the futility of simply telling others what to do. Christian organizations are not immune from system fatigue syndrome or hard times.

Sometimes kick-starting the healing requires a frank and clear assessment of the problem. The more opaque the situation, the more necessary is a process of analysis. Think of your SFS as a true systems problem and begin breaking it down to bite-sized pieces.

It can be helpful to create a scale that measures depth of pain as we confront practices, policies, cultures and histories that kill the spirit of a leader and shut down the aspirations of responsible followers. Try assigning a number from one to ten, as your physician might ask when you complain of physical pain. System fatigue may create simple indigestion or serious institutional "dis-ease." With the former, solid change management may be sufficient to meet the challenge, but, in the latter, without life-changing interventions, the symptoms can be fatal.

RESPONSIBILITY

Responsibility remains so fundamentally a core factor in leadership that our inability to tap into its power and clarity generates managerial dissonance. Even if another person refuses to take responsibility, we still have a moral, ethical and managerial template to understand the problem. SFS is often diagnosed initially when no one individual seems to be involved or aware of the significant dysfunction. Individuals neither take responsibility nor assign it; there is simply no one home to respond to the situation. An action or response that should have been carried out rings true but only after the fact, in hindsight, within the circle of participants and observers. Things fall through the cracks and mission gets swallowed up in to-do lists of urgent but unimportant matters. SFS gives us no place to assign responsibility and no basis to figure out why something is not working.

The following sections illustrate several sources of SFS in organizations. While not all link up to Paul's management challenges in Corinth, they provide useful ideas for other leaders attempting to fit this slippery water balloon in a defining box.

Policy power. Policy power can be effective but sometimes lethal. Certainly, policies are necessary in ordering the shape of an organization by communicating and standardizing important work processes and procedures, but we all know that abuse is a constant danger. A low-level employee can serve as a formally or self-appointed guardian of policy, brokering interpretations in sometimes unpredictable (or even self-serving) ways, especially when the policies become difficult to track down by their victims, who can be internal or external. Sometimes it is simply the potential to say no. The time then required to solve the problem bogs the manager down to the point where the costs of staying in the plodding dialogue outweigh the benefits of actually fixing the issue. If a manager sticks with the problem she may be seen as overbearing or bullying and the recalcitrant staff member as a victim. Some junior staff become experts at this sort of manipulation and often win in the end. Alternatively some managers become organizationally famous for the "ask forgiveness later" strategy. In most situations this only works over the short term. Someone somewhere within the system will create the perfect policy to shut down even this creative solution.

Policy power obfuscates, delays and discourages, but can eventually be challenged by either finding and clarifying the elusive policy or appropriately rewriting it within the system. But this takes time and effort and sometimes high-level intervention to fix it.

Gatekeeper power: Dragons at the gate. The gatekeeper label applies especially to those who control access to executives, the omnipotent "dragons at the gate." College presidents and CEOs can live a stress-free life if they have chosen a good dragon. This staff role often assumes the authority of the office and in most situations is a necessary practice (but possibly risky for the dragon). Some filtering functions are useful in every organization and the executive needs to maintain priorities and direction. A good dragon supports priority setting by taking on delegated decision making from the executive. If transparency and responsibility are maintained, all is well.

Some leaders hide behind their dragon and the resulting power confusion becomes pronounced. When the dragon becomes authoritarian, however, and the ambivalent leader ducks the decision, it becomes difficult to determine where the decision will come from (or even whether there will be a decision). This is where SFS emerges because the power becomes unfocused and ground fog forms. In some cases two (or more) parallel decision makers end up confusing the scenario and blurring the onus of responsibility.

A well-known president nurtured "Jane," his powerful dragon, for decades. Commonly understood to be an executive secretary, she ran the institution for his entire tenure, though equally competent and very senior executives served with him. Charismatic in a crowd, the president was an introvert and avoided relationships. While a certain distance is required in any senior leader role, this president fundamentally could not relate. Jane the dragon, a fearsome person in her own right, could slay an administrator with a raised eyebrow. The disconnect perceived by followers created chronic system fatigue in the organization. Neither the president nor Jane could be assigned responsibility for actions when the ground shifted. This kept subordinates off balance and the organization stagnant; but Jane relished the power and the president could avoid unpleasantness. SFS reigned far too long.

In another organization, the senior executive maintained a dragon stable of four staff members who had vague titles with clerical overtones but single-handedly held the entire organization hostage. Because power drifted between five different people—the executive plus his four assistants—his large domain wallowed in petty reports and low-level administrative email exchanges. It was never clear which staff member was behind the power transaction. It became apparent, however, that the executive believed that the internal buzz of even minor administrative activity, rather than external results, justified the organization's existence. An unusual business model masked these toxic activities, and because of its niche, not even the market could hold this company accountable.

Most dragon abuses show up eventually, and a good senior executive will either accept it or institute change. But the senior secretary or administrative assistant in this role navigates carefully and treads a perilous path at times. When the leader uses staff to create and perpetuate gatekeeper dysfunction, it becomes a moral and ethical issue as well.

Silo power. Silos are typified by picturesque cylinders towering next to barns used by farmers to store bulk quantities of grain and other materials. It is unclear how the term showed up in discussions about business and management, but the visual schematic of several of these standing next to each other rather graphically illustrates a lack of horizontal connection. This image works for organizations where internal groups communicate little or not at all with each other, leading to inefficiencies, loss of perspective and system dysfunction.

According to Lauren Johnson, silos are "inward-focused, self-protecting business units whose thick walls hinder collaboration and slow execution."[3] Lencioni says they are "nothing more than the barriers that exist between departments within an organization, causing people who are supposed to be on the same team to work against one another."[4] Specific resources controlled by these discrete organizational units then become difficult to access, and progress bogs down.

Sometimes well-intentioned decentralization inadvertently generates silos.[5] As we rush toward "flat" organizations, our haste to grant greater decision-making power deeper in organizations sets the stage for departmental self-absorption on internal issues while neglecting an external results orientation. Decentralization won't work without a strong outward orientation and mission discipline.

Interestingly, one of the culprits can be a support function— the very departments tasked with serving the key objectives or results of a business or organization, such as information technology (IT), human resources (HR) or accounting. In somewhat perverse ways, workers inside these particular departments can find meaning in the "we/they"—insiders and outsiders— dynamic created by silos, especially as they control access or processes required by all other workers. Aspirations toward a sense of belonging—surely a natural need in any organization— contribute to this element, showing their dark side.

Paul clearly had his hands full with the factions in Corinth, which sound remarkably like modern-day silos. Different groups within the church refused to cooperate with each other and abdicated too readily to certain ineffective leaders. In response, Paul stepped back into the vacuum and redefined reality for the group. By seeking to renew relationships, provoking the Corinthians to give generously to the Macedonians, challenging the self-absorbed culture of the city and, essentially, reintroducing a theology of the kingdom, Paul called the Corinthians back to mission, to the "meaningful Outside" (which, rather than the internal operations—which are only costs—of an organization, should be the proper focus of energy and attention on external results).[6]

Beware if you are a leader who creates silos to demonstrate

short-term results. Stirring up we/they confrontations does bond the team together, but at a long-term price. Sometimes creating a sense of urgency or a minor crisis gets people moving. But if this happens at the expense of a larger sense of unity or shared purpose within the organization, you will have a price to pay in the end.

In one case we studied, an organization had its silos so deeply embedded that they became the de facto culture of the organization. This was the result of a complex, many-layered series of factors, accumulated over a relatively long period of time, but the silo effect was primarily influenced by a leadership vacuum. The care and feeding of the silos at times superseded the mission and external results that would have produced growth and revenues. Within each silo, toxic followers sought silo goals, with little or no accountability to customers, mission, results or the meaningful Outside. The inmates truly ran the asylum, and the niche market they competed in permitted continuity longer than it should have.

In extreme cases silos can become fortified or even *Balkanized*. Fortification is a consequence of blaming and can lead to extreme silos that become their own worlds, even separate realities within alternative universes, if such a thing is possible. The organization may already be a "community of systematic self-delusion," but when the silos within the organization create yet new layers of delusion, the possibilities are nightmarish.

Fortification often involves what should have been a support function but has morphed into a power center of mission hijacking and hostage taking. In universities some registrars exercise inordinate power, as can tenured faculty, who have the time and opportunity to endlessly discuss theory or process. Garden-variety, passive-aggressive silos merely create dead areas of ineffectiveness and irrelevance. When war breaks out between Balkanized silos, in the absence of leadership, the inter-silo combat can bury the organization in this "silage."

In silos, top management should invariably take responsibility, because this is where direction is set and working relationships clarified. But, at the same time, without a clear sense of the business or mission of an organization vigorously and insistently communicated and measured on a regular basis, silos will naturally emerge.

A FINAL THOUGHT

"For our struggle is not against flesh and blood, but against the rulers, against the authorities, against the powers of this dark world and against the spiritual forces of evil in the heavenly realms" (Ephesians 6:12 NIV). Sometimes we have to look beyond personalities to the spiritual forces that are taking advantage of a person's weaknesses or institutional preoccupations or misconceptions. That does not mean letting the individual or the organization off the hook, but it offers a different perspective, one that looks at systemic issues as well as persistent ones that defy logic or resolution.

Benign, structured and intentional decentralization may find its counterpart in an organizational sin of omission—leadership vacuums at the top that evolve toward toxic ambivalence. The absence of direction—whether derived from unwillingness of a leader to get involved, fear, simple incompetence or the intentional ignoring of embryonic silos—leads to dysfunction. When dragons or policy power are involved it becomes more difficult to identify a responsible individual. When left on their own, toxic followers can quickly capitalize on a leadership vacuum, and powerful silos result.

Before getting to the positive and more hopeful possibilities, including the solutions we are proposing for battered leaders, more background on the unique environment presented by battered leaders is sketched out.

TOOLBOX

Sometimes it can be cathartic to write out the reasons why we feel distressed. You might even come up with a list similar to Paul's below. There are some Christian leaders today, working in hard places, who are actually going through some of the same trials Paul experienced.

- Conflict in Corinth
- Disappointing friends
- Problem person
- Wearing masks
- Playing games
- Maneuvering and manipulating behind the scenes
- Battered by troubles
- Spiritually terrorized
- Things falling apart
- Beaten up and left for dead
- Jailed
- Mobbed
- Working hard, late, without eating
- Blamed
- Slandered
- Distrusted
- Ignored by the world
- Rumored to be dead
- Immersed in tears
- Living on handouts
- Having nothing
- Hurt
- Exploited
- Taken advantage of
- Distressed
- Flogged
- Shipwrecked
- Adrift on the open sea
- Fording rivers
- Fending off robbers
- Struggling with friends and foes
- Danger from desert sun and sea storms
- Betrayed by brothers
- Drudgery
- Hard labor
- Sleeplessness
- Cold
- Naked

- Daily pressures and anxieties of churches
- Humiliation
- Running for his life
- Abused

- Accidents
- Opposition
- Bad breaks
- Accused of fraud

How does Paul handle hard times? What is the appropriate response for me as a leader when I encounter hard times?

On the other hand, if you try this, you might realize that your list does not appear to be quite as painful as Paul's. In either case, read the following Scriptures and rephrase them in your own words to remember how God, referred to as "Father," comes alongside battered leaders.

> He comes alongside us when we go through hard times, and before you know it, he brings us alongside someone else who is going through hard times so that we can be there for that person just as God was there for us. (2 Corinthians 1:4)

> Praise be to the God and Father of our Lord Jesus Christ, the Father of compassion and the God of all comfort, who comforts us in all our troubles, so that we can comfort those in any trouble with the comfort we ourselves receive from God. (2 Corinthians 1:3-4 NIV)

> We have plenty of hard times that come from following the Messiah, but no more so than the good times of his healing comfort—we get a full measure of that, too. (2 Corinthians 1:5)

> For just as we share abundantly in the sufferings of Christ, so also our comfort abounds through Christ. (2 Corinthians 1:5 NIV)

Since God has so generously let us in on what he is doing, we're not about to throw up our hands and walk off the job just because we run into occasional hard times. (2 Corinthians 4:1)

Therefore, since through God's mercy we have this ministry, we do not lose heart. (2 Corinthians 4:1 NIV)

These hard times are small potatoes compared to the coming good times, the lavish celebration prepared for us. (2 Corinthians 4:17)

Therefore we do not lose heart. Though outwardly we are wasting away, yet inwardly we are being renewed day by day. For our light and momentary troubles are achieving for us an eternal glory that far outweighs them all. (2 Corinthians 4:16-17 NIV)

People are watching us as we stay at our post, alertly, unswervingly . . . in hard times, tough times, bad times. (2 Corinthians 6:4)

We put no stumbling block in anyone's path, so that our ministry will not be discredited. Rather, as servants of God we commend ourselves in every way: in great endurance; in troubles, hardships and distresses. (2 Corinthians 6:3-4 NIV)

PART TWO

PARTICULAR CHALLENGES

5

Is "Christian Organization" an Oxymoron?

Organizations, in their essence, are not and cannot be Christian."
This theory follows on the tail of endless conversations, interactions and management transactions with friends, colleagues and total strangers who work (or used to work) for "Christian" organizations. In many cases, these dialogues involved refugees from these organizations, dealing with their own hurt and cynicism. We recall the comment by a respondent quoted earlier, "Some of the best people I know used to work for (an unnamed large 'Christian' organization)."

It could be that we have unreasonable expectations for these organizations. In the end, the key may be the Christians who work in these organizations. Christian outcomes might be moral and ethical behaviors that result from the Christians acting Christianly, who inhabit these organizations. But, of course, Christians don't have a monopoly on moral or ethical behaviors. How would a Jewish or Muslim manager with deep moral convictions behave any differently from a Christian manager? Or a Confucian or Buddhist manager, for that matter?

Much of the basis for how we think about moral and ethical behaviors emerges from the Old Testament—with much in common among the three historic Abrahamic faiths when it comes to ethics and morality. So is there a Christian manager who embodies New Testament behaviors that would differentiate her from a Jewish or Muslim counterpart? (We might argue that there are some practices and behaviors that do so, but that is the subject of another book!)

Can a Christian organization be "saved" in some sense? Most would agree it couldn't. Salvation involves the meeting between God and the individual in, through and because of Christ. There are other words we would use to describe that relationship, such as *redeemed* or *consecrated*. These work for individuals but not for organizations. Can an organization sin? Again, probably not, though individuals in organizations certainly can and do, sometimes with great proficiency.

A recent study claims that organizations may now suffer from any of forty-one separate illnesses or pathologies.[1] Apparently, in a fascinating act of anthropomorphism, a dozen medical doctors were consulted to get the terminology right. While it is tempting to assign attributes like illness, pathology or sin to organizations, it creates confusion. By contrast, at the time of the Corinthian case study, organizational life was intimate and could simplify dealing with individuals; there did not seem to be a strong agenda for assigning a separate identity to the Corinthian organization.

But surely the church at large, the body of Christ, must be more than a mere organization. Many of the powerful realities of the body and the church exist in the heavens, or as Dallas Willard might say, just next to us, almost here, but not quite.[2] From time to time there may be ways we see this more clearly, but not always. These are *real* realities, but they are just not necessarily comprehensible with the human tools we presently possess. Sacraments seem to operate this way—the inward and invisible grace exists, but we can't necessarily point it out to someone else; only the outward and visible sign can be seen. A local church embodies the deep reality of the global church and is surely, in some sense, the body of Christ. Yet at the same time, it demonstrates many, if not all, attributes of organizations.

Max De Pree once reported to his denomination that organization was neither theological nor sacred. And, quite frankly, there are some obvious blemishes that keep popping up. To separate the annoying and fleshly results we sometimes observe from the purity of the kingdom reality strays close to gnosticism. Understanding the kingdom is not always a simple task.

So the local church can be the church, and it can also be a neighborhood organization, invariably with spots and wrinkles. Bottom line: any church or nonprofit, or even business, with Christians involved, which aspires to be "Christian" or embody Christian values, will be vulnerable. And any Christian involved in these organizations can end up as victim or culprit, depending on the scenario.

SOME BRIEF BUT VALUABLE CHURCH HISTORY: SODALITIES AND MODALITIES

Ralph Winter, in a now-classic article,[3] identified Christian organizations as either *modalities* or *sodalities*. His discussion is a starting point for thinking how Christians organize themselves for vocation and outreach. Winter tried to resolve the problem plaguing many parachurch (nonprofit) organizations by recalling the Catholic confraternities generally emerging from monastic orders in the Middle Ages.[4] These organizational forms help reconcile long-standing tensions between local churches and parachurch organizations.

As the medieval church evolved, many of the great monastic

houses became a law unto themselves; this created strained relationships with local bishops and parish priests.[5] Notice that this revolves around who is in charge and how leadership will be exercised. The monastic orders reported to senior officials in Rome, and the parish/diocesan structure existed within a different system of bishops, archdeacons, archbishops, cardinals and so on. At times, the monastic orders had a direct line to the pope, (probably a troubling experience for the local bishop and even a few cardinals in Rome). The Catholic concept has become quite sophisticated but it helps explain tensions within the Protestant denominations, particularly as the missionary movement began in the late eighteenth and nineteenth centuries.

The missionary societies were supported by local church structures but gradually operated quite independently from them. As they drifted away from the founding denominations, they became totally separate organizations, from which evolved some of the largest and most influential nonprofits in the world, including a multinational nongovernmental organization (NGO) like World Vision and youth movements like Young Life or InterVarsity Christian Fellowship. From time to time the tensions resurface over issues of faith and practice. Leadership and management practices have taken on different forms within these, with sodalities fostering new and innovative forms of operation and organization.

In Corinth these organizational precursors are evident. Paul and friends, on an extended trip setting up churches around Asia Minor, form the classic and original missionary band (or sodality, in Winter's terminology), establishing *modalities* in various places. For the gospel to advance, functioning organizations, well managed and led, must be planted and nurtured in far-flung places. The impetus to sustainability must be locally driven and established in a way that continuity would not require further outside interventions. In short, Paul needed a successful franchise operation.

Tensions abound, both with the home modality—the Jerusalem elders—and with the newly installed but demanding leadership in the new modality in Corinth—the faltering franchise Paul is attempting to manage. Paul is in the middle of two modalities, leading without power, struggling to find common ground to ensure the long-term sustainability of the Corinthian franchise.

Part of the battered leader's problem is organizational, highlighting the turbulence that structural issues create. In examining modalities and sodalities we should note that each has internal power, accountability and authority structures that usually work, even if relationships might be strained between the two organizational forms. Though some aspects of sodality are present in Paul's enterprise, a key theme is his lack of conventional authority to challenge their issues; they have simply denied him the right to lead. A major portion of the case emerges from his search for a common platform that reestablishes the appropriate direction for them to pursue.

Hoping to bypass traditional tensions between modalities and sodalities, we suggest that the church can come in a variety of forms, all bringing with them unique challenges to leaders and managers. New forms, including communities of practice that test traditional systems by diffusing power and flattening hierarchies, still suffer their own set of behaviors that can bring down those exercising leadership. Their genius, however, is that they stop functioning the instant someone tries to own or control them. The community of practice has the potential to be a place where the purest form of leadership—leading without power—comes into play.

Communities of Systematic Self-Delusion

One morning at 4:00 a.m., after a few months of consulting with a particularly complicated organization, Wesley realized that he truly had fallen down the rabbit hole, finding himself either in Alice's Wonderland or in a parallel universe. It became clear that this organization had so closed itself off from benchmarking with normalcy that he could no longer share even common organizational language to describe and remedy the different situations it faced.

Far too frequently we observe organizations or even small groups gone amok. Essentially straightforward decisions "go south" in dramatic ways, even though a group of wise people gathers together to make them. At times these groups turn out to be long-standing, collegial workgroups. This is a central factor in the definition of groupthink (discussed in a previous chapter). The team members may be highly competent and technically qualified experts, as in the case of the Space Shuttle Columbia disaster. Yet in each situation, a mix of factors drives perceptions and outcomes in the wrong direction. When saddled with the added cumulative effects of organizational or system dysfunction, poor external leadership and corporate passive-aggressive behaviors, the negative reinforcing loops identified by Peter Senge (see below) take over.

Reality-Based Communities

Recent political and social events have given rise to the term *reality-based community*, to suggest that a person's opinions should be based more on accurate and observable fact than on faith, assumption or ideology; solutions should emerge from judicious study of discernible reality. Faith and belief are critical components of a person's ideology and form the basis of many of our assumptions. However, when working in an organization, members must know and understand the reality within which the company operates. Where organizations fail to carefully consider outside opinions, apply factual analysis and critically assess information, they are what we call *communities of systematic self-delusion* (CSS-Ds, for short). To be a community of systematic self-delusion a group must not only be dysfunctional and ineffective but also sustainably so, with regular mechanisms for reinforcing denial and comforting misinformation deep within the fabric of relationships. It must be partially or completely cut off from outside forces that might help it remain healthy.

CSS-Ds go beyond groupthink and are both dangerous and perverse. The complacent culture can be so deeply embedded that it becomes calcified, with little hope for operational management and leadership effectiveness. Our later discussion of organizational culture provides some background, but this phenomenon may lie even deeper than culture. Effectively, these communities seem to have lost contact with the outside world. They are not open to comparisons.

The market is a simple taskmaster—you stay in business or you don't. In management we use terms like *benchmarking* and *best* or *good practices*; businesses competing in the marketplace aggressively pursue comparisons with others because it sharpens their edge, makes them more competitive and increases profit and value. Communities of systematic self-delusion, on the other hand, simply embrace their own reality and cling to it. They resist benchmarking or the best practices of similar organizations because they focus solely on the purity of their mission and forget the disciplines of good management.

In some cases, organizational self-preservation trumps a mission that is no longer relevant. Instead of engaging in hard thinking about why the organization exists when faced with new challenges and the requirement to change, members grasp at what will keep them alive or preserve a comfortable status quo in the short run. If the members also provide the funds that keep the organization alive, the entity takes a giant step away from outside accountability and the market forces that might affect its functioning. Any time the means of sustainability diverge from the mission, the organization is vulnerable to losing its way.

Businesses can find themselves in this position, but only temporarily, when they fail to innovate in time. The problem is caught too late when cash flow slows to a trickle. The lead time to bring in a new product becomes greater than the supply of cash or receivables remaining. Sooner or later, the system catches up. It is only a matter of time.

The Corinthian church had become a community of systematic self-delusion. The membership could pool enough resources to be sustainable, and its mission and activities became whatever the group, led by the super-apostles, determined. They were unwilling to listen to the voice of the one (Paul) who knew them and their situation best. The Corinthian organization thus floundered in disarray, as a consequence of culture, factions, cliques, bad leadership, corporate impulsivity, misperceptions of wealth, poor decisions, rebellion, mobbing and any number of other factors. This community through inattention and plain contrariness transformed itself, and not in a good way.

Social sector organizations are more prone to linking delusion with sustainability and soldiering on, despite all odds. As long as its donors write checks that don't bounce, the organization stays alive, no matter how misguided or disconnected from realities. Alternate universes are filled with organizations like these that will survive generations into the future.

COLLECTIVE WISDOM

James Surowiecki produced a fascinating analysis of a related phenomenon in *The Wisdom of Crowds*.[6] He discovered that a key factor in poor decision making was a lack of private, independently acquired information. When individuals came up with their own perspectives on a situation (even if it might be wrong!), then *aggregated* these (as opposed to reaching consensus or voting), their collective wisdom invariably outperformed other forms of decision making.

Cass Sunstein, formerly at the University of Chicago and then with the Obama administration, explains *The Law of Group Polarization*: "A bunch of people who agree with each other on some point will, given the chance to get together and talk, come away agreeing more strenuously on a more extreme point." This might be the *congregated* alternative to Surowiecki, demonstrating the peculiar massing common to mobs: "If this tendency has a curdling effect on intellectual debates, it can have a downright menacing effect when the point of agreement is that a particular colleague is a repugnant nut job."[7]

CSS-Ds thus reflect the dark side of collective wisdom and involve long-term patterns of conflict avoidance, fear, groupthink, dependent decision making, improper persuasion, information cascading, power dealing and toxic relationships masked by passive-aggressive behaviors that repeat vicious cycles through a surprisingly broad range of environmental inputs. Even change and crisis may not affect their activities, and rather than seizing opportunities in crises, these organizations passively allow external circumstances to solidify their operations still further.

REINFORCING LOOPS

P. M. Senge's concept of reinforcing loops helps explain the peculiarities of CSS-Ds.[8] Building on something that can be either vicious or virtuous circles but taking the concept several steps deeper, his research shows that these loops can gain power with each iteration, generating an even more difficult challenge for resolution, as a situation digs an even deeper hole. Crisis and emergency management cases provide illustrations of this.

A crisis always begins in a certain context where vulnerability to a hazard creates risk. In Senge's examples a "balancing loop" is required to break the momentum of a negative reinforcing loop and redirect its movement more positively. Paul throws a classic balancing loop into the mix with his leadership intervention in Corinth by challenging them "to take responsibility for the health of the church" (2 Corinthians 2:9). Later he's glad that they "were jarred into turning things around" (7:9).

When you pilot an airplane, you learn the terror of spins. Virtually any flight attitude can lead to a spin, and in some aircraft designs no recovery is possible. More to the point, the pilot must carry out specific and counterintuitive actions to live. In a former life, Wesley piloted helicopters professionally, where he learned that when the engine conks out and a helicopter begins to fall out of the sky, the precise motions that usually make the rotorcraft go up will only worsen the situation.

For CSS-Ds, the right balancing loop generally involves external management activity. E. H. Schein believes that leadership is the creation and management of culture, and that leaders must step outside culture to adapt it.[9] Structural validation—essentially, consistent support by senior management—is necessary for the intervention to be sustainable. This is especially daunting, because CSS-Ds flourish best when external leadership is absent or flawed. Decisions are *congregated* rather than aggregated within the group to begin with. When leadership is not exercised a toxic CSS-D can be sustained indefinitely. Without structural validation even a temporary leadership intervention will fail. Change and crisis inevitably exacerbate these situations.

TURBULENCE

Recently we saw an ad in a magazine that got our attention: "Joe Smith didn't know that a heart attack would save his life." In the same way, many managers and leaders don't understand that change or a crisis can save their organization as well as their professional lives and reputations.

Fear is rational, because pain is always associated with change and crisis. We're not stupid when tempted by denial, self-delusion, flight or any of the other common responses to troubling events and experiences (though a friend of ours accurately introduces his crisis management lectures with the signature phrase "stress makes us stupid"). For those of us who have survived change and crisis in its myriad personal, organizational, public and natural forms, the scars and traumas can continue. The continuum of events can run from an unhappy conversation with a colleague to actual combat in wartime.

We can be hurt most badly, whether victim or crisis manager, because of our lack of control and the feeling of dread for the immediate future. It is no wonder, then, that manager and leaders can feel battered by change and crisis. We use this word carefully, recognizing that psychological and emotional trauma can be just as devastating as serious physical pain; we find unanimous agreement among those who have shared their experiences with us.

When organizations enter change and crisis, they tend to take different forms. For the most part, these transitions seem to be inadvertent, if for no other reason than the organization in question did not plan for change or crisis. The resulting organizational form may be more a reflection of the degeneration process than the adoption of a structure intentionally designed to create continuity.

CULTURAL DISTINCTIONS

Organizational and corporate cultures affect purported "Christian" organizations just as they impact other organizations. There has been an enormous amount written on culture within organizations, to the extent that sometimes culture is the explanation for almost everything. "The collective programming of the mind that distinguishes the members of one organization from another" frames one definition.[10] Other authors argue that "one of the most decisive functions of leadership is the creation, the management, and sometimes even the destruction of culture."[11] In addition, "if the group's survival is threatened because elements of its culture have become maladapted, it is ultimately the function of leadership to recognize and do something about the situation."

Schein writes:

As leaders who are trying to get our organizations to become more effective in the face of severe environmental pressures, we are sometimes amazed at the degree to which individuals and groups in the organization will continue to behave in obviously ineffective ways, often threatening the very survival of the organization. As we try to get things done that involve other groups, we often discover that they do not communicate with each other and that the level of conflict between groups in organizations and in the community is often astonishingly high.[12]

The mysteries behind many peculiar behaviors in organizations and groups can be explained using Schein's concepts of culture.

Cultural resistance to change is faced at levels beyond rational comprehension. In an even more distinctive way, culture within faith-based and especially "Christian" organizations plays a role. Faith-based entities bring unique characteristics to the workplace, adding new dimensions to the already complex operation of organizational culture.

One key factor lies in the motivation and incentivization of employees. Quite simply, it is highly unlikely that they join for large salaries; rather they are motivated by the opportunity for meaningful service, fellowship with other like-minded people, a need to participate in something bigger than they are, or to honor God. This high-mindedness can be abused by senior managers and boards who offer low pay, poor working conditions or harassing behaviors for this largely selfless-oriented audience.

Another category involves workers in faith-oriented organizations, including the church, who anticipate that these places will be "sin-free," or at least kinder and gentler than more worldly institutions. They often find that either a thin veneer of niceness or a vaguely passive-aggressive patina of denial hide deeper problems. There is no escape from the infinite possibilities inherent in mobbing, bullying, ambivalence or other toxicities, just as there is no real basis to claim that an organization itself can be Christian.

Transparency, especially in money matters, may be complicated. Salaries and salary disparities may be hidden under layers of secrecy. Most nonprofits beyond a certain size must file an annual Form 990 with the Internal Revenue Service (IRS); this pierces the veil of top executive pay, bringing some issues into the sunlight. Churches do not have to file this form, however, and in our experience (and sadly, according to frequent press reports), they can become adept in creating mazes of compensation. In some ways public sector organizations (generally not sin-free either) are required by law to hold to much higher standards of disclosure and transparency, removing one source of contention among employees. Yet part of the culture in faith-based organizations can forgive even grossly unfair pay differentials in support of the group's heavenly orientation.

NICENESS

A culture of niceness pervades the various management transactions and relationships in these organizations. While it is entirely a good thing that courtesy and civility attend our day-to-day work, niceness can be used to apply unfair standards and gloss over vulnerabilities. Passive-aggressive organizations (see below) employ niceness to avoid healthy confrontation and positive conflict. Every organization—whether faith-based or not, whether "Christian" or the Elks Lodge down the street—needs tools to resolve conflict. For many, the fear of losing a job trumps rightful challenges to bad behaviors or practices in an organization. The fear of being seen as a complainer or even whistleblower quashes many situations where a little righteous anger might be helpful. And God help the leader who allows followers a glimpse of actual frustration or negative emotion in nice organizations—gossip and mobbing may quickly ensue, and a ride out of town sometimes follows.

Often Christians hope to transfer a happy small-group experience in a healthy church to employment at a faith-based organization. Prayer, Bible study, personal support and friendships that are part of that experience are projected to their expectation for the "Christian" organization. Weekly or daily religious services at the organization, though well-intentioned and often positive, can perpetuate this ideal. Just as an employee's church may truly be a sanctuary in every sense, the employee transfers this expectation to the organization during the week. However, the expectation that the faith organization will be a place to belong, celebrating the same strong fellowship that may thrive on a Sunday morning at church, is unrealistic.

Sadly, even the Sunday morning experience of the parishioner in the pew may be very different from that of the church's leadership team, which may experience pettiness, meanness or worse. Certainly, God is able to transcend bad leadership and followership, whether in churches or other faith-based organizations, but this does not mean that the culture should not be confronted when bad behaviors are present.

Redirecting or even destroying an inappropriate organizational culture is possibly the hardest task a leader faces. Not only is this change management at its most dramatic level but also it directly challenges those systems best at fatiguing and battering a leader. Culture lies far below the visible layers and group behaviors and therefore its transformation is one of the most difficult tasks of the leader.

Passive-Aggressive Organizations

"Passive-aggressive" describes the "quiet but tenacious" resistance of an organization to direction by senior managers.[13] Processes and policies that do not work may be more to blame than individuals. Increasing complexity as an organization grows may complicate responsibility and blur accountability expectations. According to a study published in the *Harvard Business Review*, three specific areas contribute: unclear scope of authority, misleading goals and "agreement without cooperation."

One highly respected and accomplished boss had an annoying habit of jumping in to rescue every project when it reached the 80 percent completion milestone. The staff working on a project assigned by him grew to expect this, became less motivated and actually stalled the process, knowing what was surely coming. When responsibility is handed over to a motivated subordinate or team, the means to solve the problem must accompany the assignment. The full and certain knowledge that authority is granted only up to the 80 percent point of task completion kills initiative in any follower. Keeping in mind the maxim that authority and responsibility must go hand in hand is always helpful.[14]

> Paul challenged the passive-aggressive orientation of the Corinthian organization: "We refuse to wear masks and play games. We don't maneuver and manipulate behind the scenes" (2 Corinthians 4:2).

The fatal triangle case mentioned in an earlier chapter involved misleading goals. The CEO who hired the middle manager had a different idea of the goal than the manager's boss. In this politicized culture a lack of goal clarification created tension between the boss and the CEO so the middle manager took the hike.

Agreeing without cooperating follows closely behind misleading goals. In the same case, everyone agreed, at least publicly, that the goals were to be followed. But passive-aggressive behaviors nixed cooperation from the start. Intel Corporation provides a healthy alternative through its "disagree and commit" practice.[15] Both the conflict and the followup action are clearly on the table. Everyone in the room, whether they agree or not, realizes that at the end of the meeting a decision will be made and all will commit, whether this brings personal happiness or not. The act of committing requires cooperation in accomplishing the goal, though the entire solution still requires a culture that buys into the practice from bottom to top. (Even "disagree and commit" would probably not have saved the manager in our example, however.)

All three factors may contribute to a situation where one leader batters another but does so in a passive-aggressive manner. Below, in response to a survey we conducted, a person describes how a work environment that had been invigorating for over four years became increasingly hostile with the hire of a new, professional employee reporting directly to the executive director. Having unclear goals, a confusing scope of work, and the refusal of the senior leader to support the team leader he brought in, contributed to a negative environment.

> Over about a six month period of time, the Executive Director's behavior became emotionally abusive and the work environment became very hostile. The things I began to observe and experience in him were his emotional abusiveness, which was very subtle at times, his lack of trust, his manipulation, his exploitation of people and power, his controlling, micro-managing behavior and his unresolved issues of dealing with women. This was particularly true for competent successful women who, on the one hand he wanted to support, promote and collaborate with, but on

the other hand he felt threatened by and so evidenced a strong need to compete and criticize them to others.

As Dallas Willard points out, "One of the things that should happen in the fellowship of Christ's people is there should be no attack and no withdrawal."[16] Frequently we own the first principle but not the second. What happens then is that we end up working alongside defensive, tense individuals, using our own emotional and mental energy just to navigate our interaction with them. Paul seems to have been well aware of the destructive realities of the societal and organizational culture he was confronting, and he uses sharp words and attention-getting actions to address them.

> You stare and stare at the obvious, but you can't see the forest for the trees. (2 Corinthians 10:7)

> I'd die before taking your money. I'm giving nobody grounds for lumping me in with those money-grubbing "preachers," vaunting themselves as something special. They're a sorry bunch—pseudo-apostles, lying preachers, crooked workers—posing as Christ's agents but sham to the core. (2 Corinthians 11:12-13)

Red Hook: A Final, Sad Case Study

Why do seemingly mature and seasoned adults, veterans of the marketplace, possessors of life skills that would make them wary of secular con men, fall for religious charlatans? The key seems to be the sort of innocent, blind trust attainable primarily in faith-oriented organizations. No faith seems immune. A twisted guru or imam seems equally competent at leading deluded followers astray.

In 2010 the *New York Times* reported on a pastor in the Red Hook neighborhood of Brooklyn embroiled in a typically tragic scenario.[17] Pastor Isidro Bolaños presented his church with a unique possibility: they could be hired to work on a project funded by World Vision.[18] World Vision has a stellar management reputation, a Christian focus and a record of transparency over decades regarding its operations around the world (albeit with a few understandable challenges along the way). The opportunity to do good is a difficult one to ignore, and a respected leader who sees in us the potential for greater or nobler contribution gets our attention. We like to follow those who call us to higher and better things or who present us with stronger possibilities for ourselves. Whatever the role and accompanying title we are given, when a new opportunity offers us the possibility of applying our skills to God's work, many religious people see this as a compelling proposition, regardless of the risk.

On the surface, the risk issues involved in Bolaños's proposition seemed reasonable. World Vision, unlike many faith-oriented institutions, has the reputation of paying a fair wage, so the salary amounts promised in Bolaños's proposal may have seemed appropriate to their corresponding tasks. Bolaños further broadened the credibility platform of his proposal by bringing other pastors onto the project (promising them, according to the *Times,* "a salary of $65,000 a year, a new Lexus and the chance to purchase a church building for $1").

Do Christians look at risk differently when God seems to be involved? In one sense, of course they do, because this is the essence of faith. We are to dare great things for God—we are called to the heroic. The great missionary stories of Paul and the Corinthians as well as the Jesuits and the nineteenth-century global journeys are full of this.

In Red Hook, families pulled up stakes and walked away from solid employment, homes, schools and friendships, and committed themselves to this special opportunity Bolaños and World Vision had presented them with. "The only reason I [invested in the project]," Luis Malagon told reporters, "was because they said it was World Vision."

Locally respected pastor + larger pastoral network + faithful followers + credible international organization = reasonable risk scenario

There is a serious disconnect in any leader-follower situation where Christian relationships are added to the mix. A call to the heroic can cover a multitude of scams. The old adage—if it seems too good to be true it probably is—gets set aside.

Had church members and other pastors checked the World Vision website, they would have spotted a disclaimer about Bolaños. As the *Times* reported, when World Vision staffers began investigating his use of their brand, Bolaños acknowledged that he did not have funding for his special project from World Vision. (He told them that his funding had come from government sources.)

The distinctive Christian culture of Bolaños's victims, cleverly manipulated by a classic shyster, conveys some of the worst characteristics of relying blindly on faith in organizations. The facts could involve any religious organization in almost any Westernized country and with any ethnic group.

By now the connection between the Red Hook "hook" and Corinth should be emerging. The red herrings of Corinth are still around after nearly two thousand years. Compare the super-apostles, deceptive messages, money issues, gullibility, denial, placid and complacent followership, rejection of painful truths, and the distinctive peculiarities of the Christian organizational scene, then take away the first-century bathrobe outfits, add a Lexus, and we have déjà vu all over again. The other church leaders in Brooklyn who began nursing local victims through the pain would find deep empathy from Paul.

An umbrella theme in the Corinthian case is how the local community manages its own sin. Every so-called Christian organization deals with sin. Key to Paul's leadership intervention is guidance to the Corinthians on how to manage the sin in their midst—the subject of the next chapter.

TOOLBOX

Read the passages below. What do we learn from 2 Corinthians about the difference between "charismatic" leaders and "transformational" leaders?

> We carry this precious Message around in the unadorned clay pots of our ordinary lives. That's to prevent anyone from confusing God's incomparable power with us. As it is, there's not much chance of that. You know for yourselves that we're not much to look at. We've been surrounded and battered by troubles, but we're not demoralized; we're not sure what to do, but we know that God knows what to do; we've been spiritually terrorized, but God hasn't left our side; we've been thrown down, but we haven't broken. What they did to Jesus, they do to us— trial and torture, mockery and murder; what Jesus did among them, he does in us—he lives! Our lives are at constant risk for Jesus' sake, which makes Jesus' life all the more evident in us. While we're going through the worst, you're getting in on the best! (2 Corinthians 4:7-12)

I hear that I'm being painted as cringing and wishy-washy when I'm with you, but harsh and demanding when at a safe distance writing letters. Please don't force me to take a hard line when I'm present with you. Don't think that I'll hesitate a single minute to stand up to those who say I'm an unprincipled opportunist. Then they'll have to eat their words. (2 Corinthians 10:1-2)

And what's this talk about me bullying you with my letters? "His letters are brawny and potent, but in person he's a weakling and mumbles when he talks." (10:9-10)

But if you put up with these big-shot "apostles," why can't you put up with simple me? I'm as good as they are. It's true that I don't have their voice, haven't mastered that smooth eloquence that impresses you so much. (11:5-6)

Since you admire the egomaniacs of the pulpit so much (remember, this is your old friend, the fool, talking), let me try my hand at it. (11:21)

If I had a mind to brag a little, I could probably do it without looking ridiculous, and I'd still be speaking plain truth all the way. But I'll spare you. I don't want anyone imagining me as anything other than the fool you'd encounter if you saw me on the street or heard me talk. (12:6)

You know from personal experience that even if I'm a nobody, a nothing, I wasn't second-rate compared to those big-shot apostles you're so taken with. (12:11)

We weren't much to look at, either, when we were humiliated among you, but when we deal with you this next time, we'll be alive in Christ, strengthened by God. (13:4)

Paul isn't a "charismatic" leader but seems to desire to be a "transformational" leader. Does he succeed?

The sociologist Max Weber defined charismatic authority as "resting on devotion to the exceptional sanctity, heroism or exemplary character of an individual person, and of the normative patterns or order revealed or ordained by him."[19] What leads us to understand that Paul is not a charismatic leader and does not intend to be?

Transformational leaders inspire followers to transcend their own self-interests for the good of the organization by engaging in a dynamic relationship. Such leadership induces followers to act "for certain goals that represent the values and the motivations—the wants and needs, the aspirations and expectations— of *both leaders and followers*." It "ultimately becomes *moral* in that it raises the level of human conduct and ethical aspiration of both leader and led, and thus it has a transforming effect on both."[20] What are the values and motivations that Paul has for the people of Corinth?

In what ways does he challenge the leadership in Corinth to transcend their own self-interest?

The Management of Sin

In business, in the public sector, and in most secular nonprofit organizations, numerous checks and balances are in place to regulate behaviors, activities and relationships. For executives who have worked across sectors, the contrasts can be startling. Managers and staff in public agencies have clear grievance procedures, ombudsmen, highly visible salary scales, unions, open-book accounting and transparent meeting laws. Business has Sarbanes-Oxley, the Securities and Exchange Commission, the IRS, the market, customers and competitors. All create and contribute to working environments with understood controls. Each functions, at least in most Westernized countries, within certain principles that convey publicly that the organization is accountable for its social impacts and that it is both ethically responsible and legally compliant. These institutions share the understanding that humans are frail creatures and, more likely than not, can act selfishly. This is especially true if the system does not impose significant controls and oversight, as well as incentives, to stimulate behaviors that are good for the group, the organization or the community. The marketplace imposes controls on business and government agencies through seemingly endless policies and regulations for transparent operations.

Trust is a critical factor. The extent to which it impacts the operation of a specific organization, however, varies based on the sector it operates in. Less trust is required of business than is required of government, and the highest level of trust is reserved for nonprofit organizations, and, in particular, faith-based entities.

The faith community establishes trust as foundational to its life together. While faith communities clearly have to comply with most laws, there is an entire realm of activity that exists beyond minimal legal and ethical requirements that sets these organizations apart. This means a different set of metrics is at work.

The most perplexing distinctive of management in the faith community could well be the handling of sin. This is peculiar to this sector and is just as peculiar to outside observers. In one sense most of the Corinthian case is about the management of sin. Try reading through, start to finish, and notice how many different approaches Paul takes in handling the challenge.

Faith communities substitute a trust/sin approach for most of the controls present in other sectors yet find that trust does not always prevail nor meet the same standards. At one level there is enormous confidence that through spiritually directed leaders and with the right "heart" the individual, as well as the organization, can achieve balance between the self and the group, and act in a way that is for the good of others. Historically and in much of the world today, there is a contrived separateness from the world—rejecting the controls, oversight and incentives embraced by nonbelieving individuals, secular agencies and public systems. In the United States we have a long history and legal basis for the separation of church and state. Yet churches and related religious entities have used this separation to hide conduct that others would find unethical, demeaning, irresponsible or even illegal. When systems of trust break down internally—whether resulting in harm, illegal actions or the slow death of external results—the culture of the faith community quickly labels the action according to its own rules. In "Christian" organizations there is a definite hierarchy of sin, with sexual misconduct being at the top of the list.

The term *fall from grace* provides a great euphemism in understanding the community's perception. The tumble taken by Ted Haggard, former president of the National Association of Evangelicals (NAE), is a case in point. A leader of a business company might unabashedly carry on a series of same-sex relationships without faultfinding by peers or the marketplace. But in the faith community, where such behavior is considered immoral or sinful, it requires acknowledged guilt (accompanied often by shaming), remorse, confession, ongoing accountability and, in some cases, eventual restoration. On the other hand, a faith community leader indulging in sins further down the hierarchy, such as greed or gossip, as destructive as the behaviors may be, is generally ignored. Such leaders may maintain grossly inequitable salary scales, unimaginable in the public sector, yet be gratefully affirmed by employees committed to the community's mission.

Not all sin is absolute—some is culturally shaped, either in nature or degree. Complicating the dilemma, workers in faith communities individually tend to have very clear but often incompatible ideas of what sin is. Their differing cultures, shaped by history, specific orthodoxies, geography and many other factors, sometimes result in sin as a fluid and shape-shifting target.

The standards established by Benedict in his *Rule of Life* (c. 530) are an example of severe expectations sustainable only in a particular context. What Benedict might consider sin could be viewed differently in another faith community. Yet the other community would have its own quite clearly recognized standards that define the breaching of trust, or sin. In some faith communities domestic violence and income tax fraud have been winked at, but "not being nice" can have cataclysmic consequences.[1]

SIN AVOIDANCE: JUST DON'T DO IT

It is quite clear that leaders should avoid sin—otherwise their moral authority is compromised and they lose their platform to speak into the lives of others. So managing sin is a central task of faith community leaders, yet one that most would not understand in these terms. Recognizing three variables can help us work out this principle in practice: (1) we all do it, (2) shame and guilt cloud the issue, and (3) sin is everywhere, diminishing performance.

We all do it. Both leader and led may sin. Consequently, there is no moral high ground for anyone. Pretending that some people are above sin creates insecurity and often a diminished desire to confront sin in others. The result is that sin is frequently relativized. The question of who exercises moral authority to make this determination therefore becomes a critical one.

If the led identify sin in the leader, using whatever paradigm or set of expectations that fits their organizational culture, they may simply deny the leader's right to lead them. If the leader challenges perceived sin in the led, the latter may decide that the workplace has become hostile, and relationships—the bedrock of the faith community—crumble into pain and confusion. When the led are allowed to create and feed their own set of perceptions, especially when triangles are allowed, resolution becomes largely a political process not tied necessarily to right or wrong. We have seen cases where an individual employee— challenged to respond more constructively to criticism by a manager or to the goals and norms set by the project team—immediately takes sick leave that then evolves into a compensation claim. This discourages the community from accomplishing the goals that the underlying trust factor is meant to restore. Individually, these are self-reinforcing pathologies; corporately, they generate communities of systematic self-delusion.

Shame and guilt cloud the issue. The use of shame and guilt flourishes in the management of sin, and it works both ways. It carries stigma for those involved far into the future—the gift that keeps on giving. Even when a reconciliation process is followed incorporating confession, forgiveness and restoration, sin only "disappears" in the eyes of God. His people have become highly adept at letting shame and guilt linger on. With individual relationships, grace, mercy, love and humility all mitigate transactional sin; but past a certain point the human ability to look the other way and turn the other cheek shuts down. There we find individuals who are mere shadows of their true selves. Genuine forgiveness this side of heaven is a very rare phenomenon, and few faith communities, especially those with significant institutional memories, pull it off well on either side of the equation.

Sin is everywhere, diminishing performance. Every organizational transaction has the potential for sin. At this stage, when the cost of overlooking or forgiving exceeds the cost of introducing resolution into the transaction, some movement may be taken toward compromise or change. However, to step into this situation becomes increasingly difficult. We have seen senior religious leaders play fast and loose with financial proscriptions and their board of directors or colleagues look the other way. Permission has been given for the conduct to continue. The rate and degree of excessive spending or personal benefit accelerates and eventually gets out of control, yet the opportunity costs of managing such sin are astronomical, so challenges wait until the situation becomes intolerable or an independent third party confronts the problem. The underlying behavior, not held in check, restricts the ability of the organization and the individual to move forward. Eventually, the system or the part most directly affected shuts down.

Devoting time and attention to defuse such situations means less time and attention is given to the purpose or mission, effectively weakening the organization's ability to perform and generate the external results it requires to survive. Paul thus succinctly and forcefully identifies the problem in Corinth as he sees it:

> I do admit that I have fears that when I come you'll disappoint me and I'll disappoint you, and in frustration with each other everything will fall to pieces—quarrels, jealousy, flaring tempers, taking sides, angry words, vicious rumors, swelled heads, and general bedlam. I don't look forward to a second humiliation by God among you, compounded by hot tears over that crowd that keeps sinning over and over in the same old ways, who refuse to turn away from the pigsty of evil, sexual disorder, and indecency in which they wallow. (2 Corinthians 12:20-21)

Though it might be convenient for followers to deadlock an uncomfortable situation with guilt-generating finger pointing, it will not fix the problem. Though all parties bring their own dirty laundry to the table, this cannot stall resolution of issues. All have sinned—failed to live up to their responsibilities, not asked for forgiveness, ignored pressing social and emotional issues of staff, to name just a few. In situations like this, what does it mean to manage sin? The answer is spelled R-E-S-P-O-N-S-I-B-I-L-I-T-Y.

This issue is covered in more detail in a later chapter, but some background on how we view management can help us begin to think about this dilemma.

> "The focus of my letter wasn't on punishing the offender but on getting you to take responsibility for the health of the church."
> (2 Corinthians 2:9)

First, Manage . . .

In general, managing refers to the act of getting people together to accomplish desired goals and objectives. Peter Drucker often said that management was making knowledge effective. If true, then managing sin means first having knowledge of what sin is in the context of our position and organization, and then exploring ways to reduce its negative force and make the opposite effective. While many of us could have an interesting discussion on what might be considered the inverse of sin, we assert that it is virtue and that the opposite of the destructiveness—personally and organizationally—of sin is the application of virtue in some form of human flourishing. To embrace this type of response is to understand that we are a mixture of both selfish and altruistic motives, that we do not judge ourselves the way we judge others, and that we are called to examine these issues in our lives.

But it starts with taking responsibility. Most of us are aware that significant issues facing our society and our world involve issues of justice and injustice. But justice and injustice happen not only on a macro level—involving nations and people groups or treatment of the weak within a system—but also on a micro level. It's what happens to you and me. Observe how people lead, manage and relate on professional levels, whether as volunteers, paid staff, executives, consultants or innovators. Individuals keenly feel issues of injustice, unfairness, bias or inequity, whether it is in the workplace, in religious communities, the classroom or where we volunteer.

No matter what roles we fill we are always working out our own issues, dealing with self-awareness and acting in concert with our understanding of self, whether consciously or not. It reminds us of the process of driving a car. Some people drive and think it is fine to keep their eyes fixed on the road in front of them. But when you are taught to drive you are told not to do that, because you can isolate your experience through tunnel vision or lack of situational awareness and not be aware of what is going on around you that might actually be dangerous.

So becoming aware of what issues we shun and why, and why we gravitate to some and not others, and how we approach daily interactions becomes a quest. If our full development as people—as God's creation—is a key part of our life's purpose, then learning and growing from these experiences is critical. This isn't easy. We can be very self-centered about these things. Janis reflects on her personal experience in these terms:

> We still live in a "comparative" world of sin—where I compare mine to yours and find you wanting. The beam in your eye is what I focus on—I do this whether Christian or non-Christian. I am offended by your "version" of sin. It can be environmental degradation, sexual addiction, body shape or poor political positioning. Whatever it is, I find you offensive and wonder how you can live your life in that state. Sometimes I hold back because I recognize it is not appropriate in our politically correct world to challenge your actions, or values or mores. But sometimes, it creeps out and I wish you would find a way to "fix"

whatever is wrong with you, and often I am willing to offer solutions or prescriptions for how you might do so.

Whatever its true, underlying cause in me—need to control, lack of trust, or sometimes even basic jealousy—it raises its ugly head and creates a divide between my soul and yours. I nurse the feelings because to do so allows me to perhaps not totally ignore my own sin—but to see it in a different light, to contrast its magnitude and effect with yours. My own lack of follow through, the way I talk about my co-worker, and what I do with my money—these I feel are insignificant in the scheme of things, especially if I keep them hidden as much as possible; I can then be "holier than thou."

SELF-AWARENESS

To create a spirit of self-awareness is to adopt a different approach. It is to include throughout the day moments of self-reflection and prayerful insight. Did I take responsibility for my actions today? Did I prioritize to accomplish real work? Did I pass up the opportunity to gossip with my coworker and criticize others on staff? In asking these questions am I prepared to wrestle with the difficulty of my own self-perception (or self-*deception*)? Can I ask those I trust to give me feedback and participate in a reality-based community? The reality is that all of this contributes either to places of human flourishing or languishing. We sometimes fail to see it, however, because of our fragmented approach.

Why do some people say, "It's not my problem," when they encounter a moral dilemma staring them in the face over which they have some control, while others get personally involved in searching for solutions? "How do some people acquire a sense of ultimate responsibility for the way things turn out?"[2] One way is aiming for "enduring objectives that motivate the person's behavior over the long haul."[3] As Gardner further explains, "ultimate concerns" help us organize our personal goals and get us working toward those interests, "promoting a profound and enduring sense of purpose for one's life."[4]

Paul tells the Corinthians to conduct a self-examination before he comes: "Examine yourselves to see whether you are in the faith; test yourselves. Do you not realize that Christ Jesus is in you— unless, of course, you fail the test?" (2 Corinthians 13:5 TNIV).

Paul asks the Corinthian Christians to consider whether they really match up in behavior with who they say they are—people in whom Christ lives. While we are often eager to examine and test others, Paul is clear that we must examine and test ourselves first. Alan Redpath similarly identifies their failure at self-examination while succeeding at attacking Paul. The goal of such an examination is never to dwell on what is wrong, the sin, but to focus attention on Christ and his Spirit that transforms us.[5]

LOVE

Love makes our judgment calls powerful and effective. It also empowers us to change. Interestingly, Jesus calls us to love others as we love ourselves.

This makes the management of sin even more complex. Not

> "What we know about God and what we do for God have a way of getting broken apart in our lives. The moment the organic unity of belief and behavior is damaged in any way, we are incapable of living out the full humanity for which we were created." (Eugene Peterson, "Introduction to Ephesians," The Message)

only are we often unaware of our sinful behaviors or our harmful attitudes, we don't always love ourselves either. What does loving ourselves look like? N. T. Wright interprets it this way:

> Jesus (echoing the Old Testament) told us to love our neighbors as we love ourselves. The first thing to note here is that he wasn't basically talking about feelings. As often in Jewish and Christian thought, love is, first and foremost, something you *do*, not something you feel; the feelings often follow the actions, not (as in some modern thinking) the other way around. "Loving myself," in Jesus' teaching, does not therefore mean what the modern therapeutic movements mean when they speak of "feeling good about myself." This may or may not be involved. What "love" means first and foremost is taking thought for someone, taking care of them, looking ahead in advance for their needs, in the way that you would take careful thought about and plan wisely for your own life.[6]

We know a young woman who faced being stalked by her pastor. At great personal and family sacrifice she confronted the man and the organization. Eventually after going through a lengthy recovery, she became healthy enough to engage again with family and a new faith community. If she did not love herself enough she could never have confronted the man and the church. Loving ourselves and then loving others is critical to managing sin.

Expressing this love is not always pleasant. Many people find this difficult because they frequently confuse love with sentimentalism. The latter, once described as "uncritical kind feelings" has little to do with justice since it is so severely limited. Sentimentalism is "kindness without conscience, sympathy without realistic assessment, goodness without reckoning."[7] Instead, our obligation is to grow into mature adulthood—"to know the whole truth and tell it in love—like Christ in everything" (Ephesians 4:15).

THE PRACTICE OF SIN MANAGEMENT

Here are three steps to figuring out sin management. Not surprisingly, there are more, because much of our Christian life is about this. But these three are a good place to start: self-examination, a crucible experience, and hearing the voices of others.

Self-examination. To embark on the practice of sin management personally and organizationally requires self-examination—using self-reflective habits. These take time to be formed in us and will generally require some cognitive decision as well as an intention to re-engage in learning, self-awareness and self-management. It means personally going in and down—inside yourself and looking at your own culpability and weakness and then seeking to apply either spiritual principles—such as the *examen* of Ignatius Loyola or the spiritual disciplines.[8] You could also engage in journaling, practice meditation or mindfulness, or attend retreats where you can disconnect from the nagging demands of the immediate situation.

Once that process is engaged and practiced regularly, we begin to develop habits—personal, business, and social—that can alter our responses to the behaviors that we consider sin in others and that cause us grief. As we become more self-aware, we can begin to expand on the emotional and social competencies, crosscultural intelligence skills and related processes that help us develop in these areas. We begin to see our own imperfections not as momentary reactions or as occasional mistakes or slip-ups—as many are prone to label them—but rather as our natural inclinations, behavior and attitudes to be reckoned with. That enables us to more honestly observe and reorient ourselves to new processes and behaviors, especially when our thinking, our position, our beliefs or our practices are challenged and we feel threatened.

Self-examination also creates the opportunity to shift our theory-in-use, or the mental model we are using, and to question and subject to critical scrutiny the underlying and governing variables.[9] The thoughts and responses in table 6.1 are one way to help us delve deeper into constructing new mindsets from which we get different perspectives on the management of sin.

Table 6.1. Self-examination

When we think . . .	We should ask . . .
I have no choice.	Can I make a difference?
No one will know.	Is it the right thing to do?
It's insignificant.	Is that true cumulatively and in the long run?
It won't hurt anyone.	Will it have unintented consequences?
No one else cares if I do.	Can I make it right?
I have a right.	Do I have a responsibility?
If it weren't for (name of person) . . .	Am I exercising relationship responsibility?
It will make me look good.	What behavior am I modeling to others?
It's my decision.	Does it fit with the beliefs and values I verbalize?

Where leaders just cannot understand their own negative dynamics or how their own mental models inhibit accurate self-perception, the issue may be that they have never really failed or allowed their failures to be useful. It is frequently the case that until that happens individuals will never appreciate their own reasonability in the havoc or dis-ease that they have sown. "Only with failure," says Tom Peters, "can you verify wrong ways of doing things and discard those practices that hinder success."[10]

Paul was not perfect—we see evidence of his sins reflected in some of the conflicts conveyed in the New Testament—but in this case study he is approaching sin management from the perspective of a leader who is, first of all, just trying to get the Corinthians' attention so they will listen to him again. Paul recognizes and responds to the issues the Corinthians raise about him—he just refuses to see them as sins or failings. Rather, for him they are the right action. In fact, Paul was in trouble with the Corinthians for *not* doing exactly what most televangelists and many pastors do today—asking for financial assistance. He was not dependent on them for his physical welfare.

Some tend to believe that doing the right thing permits passive sailing through life, waiting for God to bring clarity: if I have taken a wrong turn, God will steer me back. We assume that God is like a car navigation system that speaks to us. When we make a mistake or take a wrong turn, God will say, "When safe, make a U-turn" or "Turn left, turn left."

But with God's guidance—as with most things in life—the more we practice being aware and obeying, the better we get at it. When we become discerning, when we care about what we hear (awareness), when we begin to process how we judge people in light of that awareness, when we lovingly put ourselves in their place (which is what Jesus did when he became human), we begin to understand things in a new light.

Realistically this requires a willingness to live in the question—listening, loving and learning while dwelling in the tension of opposing forces of accountability and grace, both for us and for others. "How we think, how we feel, how we evaluate internally is as important to ethics as is conforming to proper ethical norms."[11] It is not a mental exercise; it is experienced with all of our personality—involving the core of who we are.

The result is that we look at office politics differently. We will see who is mistreated and take action when wrong prevails; we will speak up on behalf of those who are less powerful. In some situations we may find that our very participation strengthens the powerful and oppresses the weak. We will discourage gossip, knowing that words can kill. We will build on what we learn from these experiences to act on issues affecting others and to develop our position on how others should be treated, even when we disagree with them.

A crucible experience. As many thoughtful leaders have observed, it generally takes a crucible experience of some kind to make us into seasoned, wise, serving individuals. It may be a spiritual quest or developmental odyssey, rigorous discipline to a demanding sport, immersion in significant responsibility such as single parenthood, or testing in war or natural disaster. These events are formative in developing in us not only fortitude but also an awareness of our own mortality and finiteness that puts our individual failures into a broader perspective. Extensive research has demonstrated that we learn best through failure, and those in our organizations who have not experienced it firsthand and sought to learn from it tend to be among the first to see a breakdown in the system as caused by the failure of others.

For most battered leaders, however, there is always the possibility that the leader did contribute at some point to the unraveling. In managing sin all should share its conviction, if necessary, while seeking appropriate resolution to the problem. The challenge is to prevent sin from stalling the solution or diluting the ability of the leader to lead, especially when toxic followers (who can be master manipulators) are present.

We know Paul found this idea helpful. That's why he sent Timothy to be his eyes and ears, as well as to communicate a message. Timothy and Titus are people Paul can count on to represent him and yet also be listeners, able to engage with those who feel slighted or mad at Paul—and to be reconcilers. They were part of Paul's ammunition to deal with the dissenters (Timothy—1 Corinthians 4:17; Titus—2 Corinthians 7:5-7).

Hearing others. The next step in the management of sin involves listening to the voices at the table. The openness and willingness to engage others in management and decision-making processes is a critical prerequisite to the type of leadership that can adapt and change.

Leadership requires a willingness and ability not only to recognize an obligation to be part of reconciling differences but *to advance change.* Without change, staying at equilibrium, we (and our organizations) are actually dying—that is the nature of our organic state.

People may not want to take sides; they may understand conflict only as a win-lose scenario with the right path lying in loyalty to the institution and obeying the rules. Some are smart enough to figure out that any other response will just create more work! So their perception of reality—as incorrect as it may be—is what they stick with. It is too threatening to let go; instead, they seek superficial solutions. There may be occasions where the leader relies on an inner voice (or for Christ followers, the Holy Spirit), and the group or team must either buy in or leave. These times should be rare; otherwise, such an attitude becomes abusive, whether intended or not. Language like "God told me" can often come from an individual who is insecure about his position.

These are difficult calls. Perhaps the worst scenario (but the most expedient for many religious people) is to create a situation so unbearable that the other person is forced to move on. This is one of the saddest examples within religious organizations and is practiced time and again. Rather than face conflict or confront our emotional and social weaknesses and problems, we claim we are avoiding conflict when, in fact, we are merely putting a different face on it. This cowardly act dumps responsibility on the individual, and the larger group or organization skates away. Chronic within religious organizations, this cop-out characterizes peace as the absence of conflict rather than a healthy intervention addressing the underlying dis-ease.

In one difficult situation, a manager went to each of his colleagues to ask honestly for feedback on his responsibility in a conflict situation. Only a few would contribute thoughts aimed at facing up to the dysfunction. In acknowledging the mistakes he had made, the manager also questioned how they might move forward. He received only one response. Within a few months the department had forced the individual out by back channeling and getting institutional support for a drastically different program that they could live with.

In a different situation, a leader who believed in empowering emerging leaders sought to encourage a new department member by giving her increased responsibilities. In the ensuing fiasco it became clear that the individual complained to a senior executive, apparently to align herself with another disaffected group she believed would be more likely to influence her career. The leader discounted the rumor of her complaint, although he eventually asked her the truth of it. She denied that the conversations had taken place, and he trusted her. However, the scenario played out, and he soon left. Several years later when this leader attended an emotional and social intelligence seminar requiring a prior 360 assessment, one responder specifically addressed this situation. He saw this as a blindness of the leader, saying the leader refused to deal with the obvious; whereas, the leader saw it as an opportunity for the other person to choose what type of person she intended to be.

Within this religious institution both the deceptive employee and the leader's boss, who listened to her, undercut the leader's ability to lead. Rather lamely, they saw themselves as averting conflict and rescuing rather than key to generating an unhealthy and demeaning situation.

Those involved in mediation note that it is very difficult for people in a conflict to reach the state of mind where one party acknowledges responsibility and admits guilt. Much conflict stems from different perspectives on an issue when in fact there is no right answer. In finding a way through the conflict there may be different options, some of which fit better than others.

What Is Resolution?

Is resolution just moving on? Institutional adjustment? Change in leadership? In what ways does the organizational culture support or diminish the process of healing or resolution? Some resolutions are difficult because they challenge the culture of the organization. Tension between institutional and personal goals can result. An individual's concern may be so significant that it surpasses institutional loyalties and forces potentially destructive actions. One of the primary remedies is the decision to take legal action. This is more likely to occur where there is no third party looking out for the interests of the less powerful or where there is no clearly stated process for resolving issues or complaints. Yet it may still evoke a feeling of being disloyal to the institution, and the discomfort may lead to either real or perceived stress and ineffectiveness on the job.

We can testify to the fact that satisfactory solutions do not always happen. A wedge develops and becomes impassable unless two things are present.

1. *A committed, long-term intervention where no one has a vested interest.* This role may be as formal as a hospital ombudsman or as informal as an impartial but influential third party. In most situations, however, the problem is that the person who pays the third party—either directly or indirectly—still believes she has the right to call the shots. And while the third party may be charged with impartiality and the right to act or decide as he sees best, the realities of human nature make this very difficult. Good and courageous people are needed in the process.

2. *Institutional memory and culture that holds individuals accountable for personal and organizational change.* Too often a person who creates dysfunction or exhibits unacceptable behaviors is merely shifted from one position to another. Complaints are swept under the rug, particularly where the person is seen as invaluable in a particular niche or has significant influence in the organization. There must be a way for tracking and holding people accountable for the messes they make.

Some would argue this is antithetical to forgiveness or, in Christian circles, to the operation of grace. At a personal level this may be true and it may require a different perspective. A Jesuit speaker we heard recently characterized annoying people as Christ disguised. This is a way of reframing personality clashes and diluting the aggravation that clouds dialogue. Some of the individuals we lead are truly annoying, irritating, infuriating and bothersome. Part of reframing requires that we try to see these people as Christ (or, at least, made in his image) and seek the best way forward in light of that.

But in organizations there is a competing demand that considers the health of the whole body, not its individual parts. Such conflict management can and does on occasion result in new understanding and significant change in the individuals and in the organization.

RULES OF ENGAGEMENT

In the military, rules of engagement (ROEs) involve how force is used in particular conflicts. Managing sin invariably involves conflict, so we need rules to resolve it.

We are at best deceived and at worst cowardly when we determine that it is not our responsibility to confront, not our job to speak out, not our Christian duty to respond to organizational culture or specific individuals who are destructive or dysfunctional. Evangelicals in particular tend to narrow the allowed issues that can be discussed.

That is not the kingdom way. In the kingdom nothing is outside the rules of our engagement. If you read Matthew's Gospel, you may be surprised how frequently Jesus confronts issues of justice. While we may remember his challenge to the moneychangers in the temple, in reality he tackled many others—involving his friends as well as his enemies. He addresses strongly not only the devil and demons, the chief priests, elders and teachers of the law but also the disciples and Peter individually, people in his home town, people in the synagogue, the rich young ruler and even some of those he healed, to name a few.

How do we know where to start? When do we speak out about what is on our conscience? We can make observations and ask questions to help us discern whether we should speak up about certain situations. For example, we may want to observe or find out whether the behavior we are concerned with forms a pattern or is a one-time occurrence. The more frequently a behavior occurs, the more likely the unjust behavior will be ongoing and the more likely it is that there is a lack of awareness of the unjust nature of the action or that the behavior is ingrained.

Sometimes in an organizational or community setting we are given choices to make among a group of behaviors or actions. We may perceive one or more of those choices to be unjust, but we know we can at least choose for ourselves and encourage others to opt for the behavior that more closely models Christlike behavior. But where our choices are blocked and we have no freedom to choose the good, we need to find a vehicle for speaking or acting to create choices.

The Mirror Test

What may for you seem unjust may for others not seem so. If you work in an organization where injustice festers and you cannot bring change, you may need to ramp up your response; in the end you either fight the system or leave it.[12]

Peter Drucker—always a keen observer of human nature—challenged his students with the mirror test: "What kind of person do I want to see in the mirror in the morning?"[13] Organizations, like people, have values. To be effective in an organization, a person's values must be compatible with the organization's values. They do not

When to Speak/Act

There is a pattern

The unjust behavior is demanded by the strong

It's institutionalized

It's done in isolation from the larger community

Speaking will affect the other's nurture

The injustice scars your conscience

need to be the same, but they must be close enough to coexist. Otherwise, the person will not only be frustrated but also will not produce results.

We need to be particularly concerned where the strong institutionalize injustice against the weak. We see this where big business—in certain historical situations and also in some developing countries today—is able to embed injustice in pay and work conditions. We may or may not be personally invested in the system; on the other hand, we may find our conscience pricked by an awareness that our own consumerist behavior contributes to certain injustices and seek to respond proactively to the social impacts of those actions.

In other settings, we become aware that the behavior we question is done in isolation from the rest of the community of which the organization or individual is a part. For example, a religious organization acts in ways that are not compatible with its spiritual tenets or a local unit of a national membership organization ignores or violates the mission of the larger organization. Alone and isolated from other members, the local unit speaks and acts in violation of its charter. Sometimes the larger organization is unaware of the local entity's behavior unless advised. Few factors in creating common ground within an organization are more important than shared, communicated and understood values.

NURTURING OUT LOUD

Another significant occasion where we need to speak or act involves when our words or actions contribute to the nurture of another. In thinking of nurture as the process of replicating learned cultural information from one mind to another, it may be that we have the opportunity—or, in some cases, a moral obligation—to inform another. There are often situations where out of ignorance, cultural background or inadequate moral development, an individual acts in ways that are harmful or hurtful to others. By speaking we may affect that person's nurture, particularly when we have a relationship with the individual that allows us to influence their development.

Each of us has defining moments—points in our lives where we know we have no choice but to speak, where to be silent is to deny who we were created to be. It is in these instances that we cannot remain silent. Sometimes we have time to prepare our response to crises such as these, but frequently they are thrust upon us and we have literally only moments to take an action or voice a veto.

A Final Thought: Two Stories

But enough of the bad news—there is hope. We have wrestled as much meaning as possible from the Corinthian case in exploring the dysfunction possible in organizations, depending on the immense creativity of the Corinthians in making Paul's life miserable. It's time to find places of hope, where battered leaders can move into new productivities and effectiveness. The following two vignettes offer examples of people who have successfully wrestled with different types of conflict or, in the words of Paul, managed sin effectively in at least one area.

The next chapters then build a basis for understanding innovative organizational solutions and identifying tools for recovery.

The first vignette comes from Jim Wallis, head of Sojourners, a national Christian organization focused on social justice issues. At the outset of a recent election season Wallis shared, for the first time, about his relationship with a prominent leader with a very different political persuasion.

The Power of Reconciliation

Bill Bright was the founder and president of Campus Crusade for Christ, an evangelical organization on campuses around the country. Motivated, above all else, by the Great Commission, Bill Bright wanted to reach every person on the planet for Christ "in this generation." Concerned about the "moral degeneration" of America, Bright wanted America to come back to God—which for him meant an ultra-conservative political agenda. Bill and I were both evangelical Christians, but we clearly disagreed on a whole range of political issues.

In 1976, Bill Bright joined a far-right member of Congress named John Conlan and other conservatives in a project to mobilize evangelical prayer and cell groups for political purposes. It was, in fact, the first attempt to create a "Religious Right" in American politics—several years before the founding of groups like the Moral Majority and the Christian Coalition.

We at *Sojourners* decided to investigate. It became the most extensive investigative project we had ever undertaken and resulted in a cover story in the magazine titled "The Plan to Save America." Bright was publicly embarrassed by our exposé and the whole experience. Though we had been scrupulously careful, backing up every fact in the story with at least three sources, Bright angrily denounced me. We invited Bright and the others involved to respond, both before and after the article was published, but they chose not to. Because we also differed on almost every political question from Vietnam to domestic issues, a bitter and public polarization grew up between Bill Bright and me.

The bad blood continued for many years. I remember a particularly painful moment one year at a dinner for evangelical leaders, when Bright again went on the attack against me in a very public way, calling me a liar.

More than two decades later, Bright and I found ourselves at yet another religious leaders' dinner. When I saw him across the room, I swallowed hard and headed in his direction. He obviously didn't recognize me after so long. I introduced myself, and he became quiet. I said, "Bill, I need to apologize to you. I was in a hotel several months ago and knew you were there too. I should have come to your room and tried to mend the painful breach between us after all these years. I didn't do that, and I should have. I'm sorry."

The now-old man reached out and wrapped his arms around me. Then he said, "Jim, we need to come together. It's been so long, and the Lord would have us come together." We both had tears in our eyes and embraced for a long time. Then Bill said, "Jim, I'm so worried about the poor, about what's going to happen to them. You're bringing us together on that, and I want to support you." I was amazed. We agreed to get together soon.

A few months later, Bill and I were again, coincidentally, at the same hotel. I called Bill and we agreed to a walk on the beach together the next morning. Bill and I shared our own conversion stories. We shared our callings and dreams for our respective ministries and how we might be more connected. Bill then astounded me, saying, "You know, Jim, I'm kind of a Great Commission guy." I smiled and nodded my head. "And I've discovered that caring for the poor is part of the Great Commission, because Jesus instructed us to 'teach the nations to observe all the things I have commanded you.' And Jim, Jesus certainly taught us to care for the poor, didn't he? Caring for the poor is part of the Great Commission!" said Bill Bright. When we got back to the hotel, Bill asked if we could pray together. We sat down and grasped each other's hands. First praying for each other, we also prayed for each other's ministries. Bill Bright prayed for me, and for the work of Call to Renewal and Sojourners. When we were finished, he said he wanted to raise some money for our "work of the Lord."

Bill, who was then more than 80 years old, soon began to get sick. I kept track of how he was doing. Then one day, I got a letter—from Bill Bright. Here's what the letter said:

My Dear Jim,

Congratulations on your great ministry for our Lord. I rejoice with you. An unexpected gift designated to my personal use makes possible this modest contribution to your magazine. I wish I had the means to add at least three more zeros to the enclosed check. Warm affection in Christ. Yours for helping to fulfill the Great Commission each year until our Lord returns. Bill

Inside the letter was a check for $1,000.

As I was reading Bill's letter, my colleague Duane Shank walked into my office. "Did you hear?" he asked. "Bill Bright just died." We looked at the postmark on the letter and compared it to the news reports of Bill's death. We concluded that writing me this letter was one of the last things that Bill Bright did on earth. Bill sent a $1,000 gift to the magazine that had exposed his most embarrassing moment more than 30 years before, as an affirmation of the ministry of another Christian leader who he once regarded as his enemy. I couldn't hold back the tears, and can't again as I write down this story for the first time.

The experience of my relationship with Bill Bright has taught me much about the promise and power of reconciliation. I will never again deny the prospect of coming together with those with whom I disagree. It is indeed the power of the gospel of Jesus Christ to break down the walls between us. Thank you, Bill. I will never forget you.[14]

In the following piece, Pastor Ken Fong explores how he came to actively promote equal opportunities for women in the church after being challenged by new learning.

A Disturbing Question and a Determined Conviction on the Treatment of Women

At the urging of one of EBCLA's (Evergreen Baptist Church of Los Angeles) deacons, I began reading *NY Times* bestseller *Half the Sky: Turning Oppression into Opportunities for Women Worldwide*. Co-authored by *NY Times* reporters Nicholas Kristof and Sheryl WuDunn (who are married to each other), it's an eye-popping revelation of how believing that girls and women are inferior to men is causing them to disappear from the face of the earth.

The ratios of male newborns to female newborns around the world is always pretty darn close to being 50/50. So why is it, when governments and agencies count the number of males and females in the world later, that there are consistently *fewer* females than males? I mean, we're talking *significantly* fewer females than males and yet, according to an old Chinese proverb, women hold up "half the sky." Girls and women are somehow disappearing off the face of the planet.

Through the CARE organization, the United Nations, and a growing "Half the Sky" movement around the globe, girls and women are being empowered to speak up and speak out, to insist that they are as valuable as any male. We heard numerous stories of even young girls who, when given access to education and protected from the perils associated with being born female in their societies, learned the laws of their countries, brought charges against the male perpetrators, and even eventually were the catalysts for shifting their culture's paradigms toward girls and women. It was truly inspirational to "meet" some of these valiant heroes who couldn't, in many cases, restore their own virginity or dignity, but pursued this as their Heroes' Journey on behalf of all other girls and women in their countries. I came home with a disturbing question and a determined conviction.

The Disturbing Question: When some Christian groups interpret the Bible as teaching that God created women to live in a male-ruled hierarchy, that they must obediently submit to male "heads" or risk violating a divine mandate, aren't they also contributing to the oppression of girls and women? I left the theater no longer satisfied with just saying, "different strokes for different folks." Even if the point is made that the Bible teaches that women are of equal value before God, if a person's being a female automatically and always means that she is overtly or subtly denied equal opportunities to learn, to lead, to teach, etc., that is oppressing her in the name of God.

The Determined Conviction: As a male whom the current Christian and societal system favors, I must take even more seriously God's challenge to steward properly whatever power I've been given simply because I am male. Rather than use it to "rule over" those who start with less power, I am more determined than ever to use it to open doors that are now closed, to provide opportunities to grow as leaders and thinkers and preachers. I've been doing this for years, but now, more than ever, I will not simply enjoy my male privileges but use them to bless girls and women who today may not have access to those same privileges.[15]

PART THREE

RECOVERY
STRATEGIES

7

Peter Drucker's
"Meaningful Outside"

Battered leaders can be self-absorbed. It is similar to being physically ill—when we have the flu it is hard to pay attention to life outside our aching bodies. We focus everything on our own pain, which is understandable. Shifting our energies to external results is a challenge for battered organizational leaders because the pain inside is all consuming. Yet, one of the fastest ways to realign is to stop navel-gazing and get back on track with the mission, the reason for existing, by focusing on, identifying and defining the "meaningful Outside."

The Corinthian group appears to be almost entirely consumed by internal efforts. This creates a fertile environment for confusion. If we page through Paul's letters, we will find how often he challenges his readers to reorient and reframe their view of the world by looking outside of themselves. For a leader struggling with a group of followers intent on working the "meaningless Inside" of an organization, refocusing on the real reasons for existing is a good idea.

> Paul uses the physical needs of the starving Macedonians to get the Corinthians looking outside themselves and focusing on where they can make a difference.

Peter Drucker coined the phrase "meaningful Outside" in October 2004, while discussing the work of the CEO with several senior executives and management scholars in Claremont, California, eventually publishing his thoughts in the *Wall Street Journal*. A. G. Lafley, CEO of Proctor & Gamble, sat in on the Claremont session and developed his own thoughts on the issue later in a *Harvard Business Review* article.[1] Numerous bloggers have picked up on the idea as well.

Interestingly, though Drucker capitalizes the *O* in *Outside*, his commentators generally do not. He was one of the most precise users of the English language we have known. At times in class he would pause for long seconds to capture just the right phrasing for the idea he was communicating. So, even in small matters like capitalizing *Outside*, it appears he is saying something specific about its significance. Like many of Drucker's ideas, we believe the concept is more complex than it seems at first and that its full value will be proved over time and in practice.

Performance and *results* are longstanding key management words. Drucker's book *Management Challenges for the 21st Century* amplifies the idea that "results of any institution exist only on the outside." Effort is the only thing "that exists inside and everything inside is a cost center." The specific function of management is "to organize the resources of the organization *for results outside the organization*." *Outside* means "society, the economy, technology, markets, customers, the media, public opinion."[2] It focuses the individual on performance or what is achieved, which is what counts, rather than on the degree of effort or attention given to the action. This requires an inordinate amount of work since we all have a tendency to want to equate effort with results, as do students who frequently complain about their grade by asserting, "I worked hard. I deserve an A." Sadly they mistake simple activity for results and performance.

We should recognize that seriously considering the meaningful Outside can be highly disruptive to the status quo and internal operations, making things even more uncomfortable than normal. This can be evident in the use of organizational technologies, in adapting to new forms of communication and in reorienting the concept of customer service.

Focus on Mission

The discussions in earlier chapters emphasize the almost constant reframing used by the apostle Paul in his correspondence with the Corinthian church. If there is a single, ultimate key answer for the battered leader attempting to bring an organization back from the brink, it is to focus on mission. When Peter Drucker talks about the primary work of top management, he starts here:

> There is, first, the task of thinking through the mission of the business, that is, of asking the question "What is our business, and what should it be?" This leads to setting objectives, developing strategies and plans, and making today's decisions for tomorrow's results. This clearly can be done only by an organ of the business that can see the entire business; that can make decisions that affect the entire business; that can balance the objectives and the needs of today against the needs of tomorrow; and that can allocate resources of people and money to key results.[3]

In all of Paul's reframing approaches throughout 2 Corinthians, he systematically calls the community back to its original mission. This moves the discussion from blaming and repositions the entire dialogue. Although the problem individuals and their assertions are addressed early on, Paul moves the discussion toward realignment from the start. By focusing on mission, the accountability part of his task seems less onerous and personal. Paul's approach is similar to a parent telling a child, "You are not bad, but you sometimes do bad things."

Many nonprofit and religious workers shy away from using the word *business*. When they use *mission* it gives a sense of taking the high road; it sounds like *missionary* or *missional*, somehow purer and nobler. *Mission* tends to resonate with purpose or even values—our cause is just and our quest is glorious. Drucker himself even conceded the use of *mission* to replace *business* when talking to nonprofit groups, but the sense conveyed in the paragraph above of business results is never meant to be absent from the discussion.

Of course, businesspeople can be a little put off by this, as if their calling is less noble—crass even. The same subtly nuanced conversation surfaces when *management* and *leadership* are used, to the extent that a cottage industry has emerged trying to differentiate the two. We use the question "What is your business?" because it helps us be more precise and less fuzzy with a focus on creating a satisfied customer or client. Objective measurement of and accountability for results are more likely than when the language of mission is used. For our purposes of exploring Drucker's three questions, however, we will use the terms *business* and *mission* interchangeably.

REPOSITIONING

"Three questions" from Drucker have challenged our students (and literally millions of others) for decades. Drucker asks simply:

- What is your business?

- Who is your customer?
- What does the customer consider value?

It sounds simple, but it is not. The questions should be worked iteratively; question two depends on question one, three depends on one and two, and one depends again on two and three. If we know our business, we can decide who our customer is with more information. If we know who our customer is, then what that person, organization or company considers to be of value will flow directly from their identity—characteristics and profile as customer. When we conclude how this value is defined, we may want to reconsider and fine tune how we originally determined what our business is. When that is done, the customer identification should perhaps be tweaked. The process can and should be repeated regularly.

When all three questions seem to be plugging iteratively along, generally in step, we have a framework for understanding the business. Of course, something might change in the competitive environment, or demographics might shift, or some market might crash or emerge. Our business must quickly adapt by reasking the three questions, reshaping the answers and moving on. To do this, we must be *nimble* and *agile*—two terms that are now almost clichés. The bottom line is this: the business must move quickly, constantly adapting, to survive or flourish.

In well-run businesses, senior managers ask these questions daily, evaluate numerous decisions against them, and process any new product or process ideas through this grid. While the second two questions shape the operation, the key strategy driver—"What is our business?"—is the prime template. Several years ago, for example, the diversification fad spooked many companies into bad acquisitions; simply asking, "Is this our business?" or "Is this really what we are good at and what we should be doing?" would have prevented unsuitable mergers and much corporate grief.

REALIGNMENT

Focusing on mission shifts our attention from finger pointing or blaming. It requires that we know our business more precisely than most nonbusiness organizations would characterize it in their mission statements. A strong theme in 2 Corinthians echoes this.

The corollary to maintaining the discipline of your business is that you have a way to remember what your business is *not*. A tightly defined mission with a strong focus is a great tool for saying no to projects you should not be doing. Each exciting new idea should be challenged by the question, "Is this what we do?" If the answer is "This is not who we are," you are almost there.

RETHINKING

A focus on the business also makes us rethink our mission and how we use it, not just speak about it. Talk about mission and mission statements abounds these days. These exercises are fine, as far as they go. Most groups working through the process of developing mission-oriented thinking are closer to effective operations than they were. But nearly all stop short of the market-based immediacy and adjustments created by intense competition that businesses face. So, we will keep asking, "What is your business?" especially when trying to drill down toward more useful applications of mission thinking.

Let us point out that, like Jim Collins, we reject the idea—"well-intentioned, but dead wrong—that the primary path to greatness in the social sectors is to become 'more like a business.'"[4] Collins goes on to identify *discipline* in these things as his real point—whether applied to businesses or social sector organizations. When we apply business language or principles to the church and other nonprofit organizations, it is easy to assume that there is a general application of all such principles to the social sector; but this is not accurate. We are not suggesting that across-the-board nonprofits should act more like businesses. Drucker himself thought business had more to learn from nonprofits than the other way around. We are, however, suggesting that nonprofits often get sloppy in focusing on mission, because competitive market forces do not press them to high performance as rapidly and ruthlessly as they might push a business into action.

Perhaps no other contribution of Drucker's is as relevant and timeless as this one. If you know your mission and the mission of your organization, and everyone else does too, you will be in large measure assured of recovering from being battered. Frequently we know it's time to move on because we wake up one morning and it's clear that who we are and what we believe we came to do in a position is no longer possible. The mission has shifted—either ours or the organization's. It's then clear that there has to be a change.

If you're in a position of power you might be able to get your organization back on track; if you're not, you may see yourself somewhere else in a short period of time. But it's important that you continue to focus on the mission as long as you can. That helps you prioritize your day, your duties, your time and your attention. One colleague describes the value of mission in these terms: "When things feel overwhelming or the future is not clear, you can hold yourself accountable to the mission. If that's changed or changing that will have to be dealt with, but, up to that point, you keep yourself sane by walking the line." Without it, we can get caught up in the personal struggles, the mobbing or gossip, the destructive thoughts or its byproducts. By staying focused on the mission, we are also much more able to look to the future and plan for results.

As a leader of an organization, the focus on mission includes tackling the difficult-to-define and painful-to-address nature of differences and conflict. Ronald Heifetz argues that today leadership means "influencing the organization to face its problems and to live into its opportunities."[5] Mobilizing people to tackle tough challenges is what defines the new job of the leader.

The Competition

Competition is not always about Toyota versus Honda or Coke and Pepsi. In a larger sense it can be anything on the Outside that makes you less effective than you want to be. Finding the competition requires interpreting information about the Outside because competitors are not always clearly identifiable.

Thinking about competition for social sector or faith organization leaders seems vaguely tacky and seedy—another one of those squalid business terms creeping into a leadership discussion. Nevertheless, this may be a useful exercise.

Len Schlesinger, president of Babson College, once told a megachurch pastor that his competition for Sunday morning attendees was not the other big church across town, but every other option for the parishioner's time during the period services were held, whether watching TV, eating at a fast-food restaurant, taking a nap or sitting in a chair and doing nothing. The value proposition has to be so compelling, so captivating, that the undecided churchgoer (customer) would choose showing up at church over every other option.[6]

So every organization, church or agency needs to think about the choices made by those they serve, which is another way of looking at competition.

WHO IS THE CUSTOMER?

Once settled on mission, every business, social sector organization, church or Corinthian community should be able to use a concept of *customer*. But it requires hard work. Again, many nonprofits, and especially religious organizations, rebel at the use of this terminology. They assume that this commercializes the message or brands the organization as profit-centered or uncaring. However, the term captures the notion that we, whether religious, social, public or business, are vying for the hearts, minds and attention of the people on the street. Anything less is to diminish the nature of the skirmish that Paul so clearly identifies for the people in Corinth and the value and personhood of the individual we want to engage. We may need to keep reminding ourselves of that uniqueness in the process.

The actual stakeholders or constituencies potentially included in the word *customer* are numerous and varied. Which ones are the real or highest-priority customers? Only so many customers are possible, because resources will be organized differently for each set, and resources are limited. Social sector organizations grapple with this often, because many options are possible. Generally in nonprofits the customer is the one for whom the service is provided. For a homeless shelter, therefore, the customer is the homeless person and not necessarily the donor who provides funds on behalf of the homeless person.

A business usually has at least two customers for a product—the wholesaler and the end user. For Proctor & Gamble, CEO A. G. Lafley identifies the consumer as the customer, although the retail purchaser is often actually buying the product. This is a fine and useful distinction, because P & G understands that the consumer probably tells the retail purchaser what to buy: "Mom, I'll only brush my teeth with _____ toothpaste." Guess which toothpaste Mom buys? Mom, too, wants to keep the consumer happy.

> It is clear that Paul has plans—plans for where he would travel and who would travel with him, how the gospel should be preached and lived, as well as plans for helping people align their attention with the demands of the gospel. They may not always work out the way he envisions them, but he generally has a fallback plan as well.

PLAN FOR RESULTS

Planning is not necessarily in vogue right now. In a world of cataclysmic events and complex social, economic and human struggles, some argue there is not enough certainty in which a person can even begin to plan. Perhaps this is true for the long term and especially true for certain enterprises, but we have found personally that plans are powerful forces. This does not mean that a person does not deviate from a plan or that at times plans should be completely thrown out, but they offer steps toward the fulfillment of vision and a means to measure progress toward goals. Sometimes we may need to conceive of a plan in terms of crisis management, when we would prefer to capture the future differently. But either way, we have found that planning helps us confront our uncertainties as well as our hopes.

We once knew someone who could create a reality by simply speaking it into being—not a prophet or a seer, just a guy who could take a questionable exaggeration, repeat it confidently like it was a fact, and suddenly people started believing him. One of his friends said he was *proleptic*. When you're hopeless, it might be nice to be able to speak a more optimistic reality into being. Sadly, most exaggerations or simple unrealities spoken proleptically eventually unravel. On rare occasions, however, a good leader can stir the energies of followers by proclaiming the right, good and true in such a way that it becomes a roadmap for a new reality.

So too, personal planning can help us confront the issues in the back of our minds and offer a framework for action. Planning is a way we can speak proleptically. It bridges dreams and actions. It not only requires hope but also proclaims it. More specifically, it specifies the materials, timeline and design of the bridge that will span those dreams and actions.

Planning proleptically begins with a credo—a statement starting with "I believe." It is aspirational; we literally inhale, taking a deep breath before leaping into something. A credo is a statement of faith. When we connect credo, faith and plan, an aspirational statement becomes concrete.

Choices suggest another planning idea—scenarios. The various future realities we might envision with a sanctified imagination can take shape differently. We can stack these for comparison and weigh the implications of each.

When we were newly married, we took a day away to dream about our life together. We wrote down what we wanted to have accomplished by certain stages in our life together. It is now amazing to discuss the things we told each other and see how many of them have actually come to pass. We may not have been correct on the timeframes (there was one item Janis lost interest in very early), but they provided an interesting way of thinking about how we would make big career decisions in a two-career marriage and what we valued (living and working crossculturally, for one).

By planning we ask these questions: Does this fit with the identity the organization presents? Is this the business we are in? Does it meet the human needs voiced within the organization? Recently, in devoting considerable effort to a plan for an organization, we observed how these efforts forced individuals to rethink not only what needed to be done but to ponder the why question behind the steps proposed. Likewise, when consulting with a product-driven and therefore bottom-line-oriented nonprofit, focusing on these questions to develop a business plan resulted in a new business model and the formation of a separate company.

But one of the most critical benefits of planning is that it drives us to action. It is "meaningless to speak of short-range and long-range plans," Drucker tells us. "There are plans that lead to *action today*—and they are true plans, true strategic decisions. And there are plans that talk about *action tomorrow*—they are dreams, if not pretexts for non-thinking, non-planning and non-doing."[7]

The Corinthian Meaningful Outside

Almost all of 2 Corinthians 8–9 focuses on framing a meaningful Outside for the Corinthians. The thread following the Macedonians in other chapters picks up the same theme, hammering away gently but persistently at the self-absorption of the Corinthian community.

The little band at Corinth was an early social sector organization meeting both spiritual and human need. As such, and like others today, it needed to be effective in using scarce resources and operating responsibly in its community. To be sustainable it had to show results. Paul was frustrated that they were caught up in superficial and unproductive debates, and following shallow and phony individuals. The Corinthians were being influenced by the triumphalist tone of those who claimed professional competency and were out to make a good show with culturally approved credentials (see 2 Corinthians 3:1-3). He spends considerable time trying to draw them back to a meaningful Outside orientation and away from division and distractions inside. He called them to the business at hand.

If you have truly been battered as a leader, a major step in your healing and in the reorientation of your followers occurs when the spotlight begins to move *away* from you. Although Paul plainly feels the pain of being battered as a leader, he is mature enough to recognize that the solution is not about him but centers around a number of other leadership strategies that actually remove attention *from* him. Understandably, in any organizational or church model, there is a need for paying attention to the internal activities and efforts of the workplace or community. In the church context, without discipling, counseling, teaching, and spiritual formation the group will not be equipped to manage their meaningful Outside. In fact, when it starts out, such a community will spend a disproportionate amount of time on those newly joining. Yet the internal efforts will be understood best after identifying and understanding the meaningful Outside first. If nothing else, the Corinthian case illustrates the cost of *not* applying a concept like Drucker's three questions to churches and faith-driven organizations.

Whatever your structure, the business (mission) and its external results drive your organizational design, your executive or pastoral activities, your budget, your plans, your prayer and meditative life, and your legacy and future impact. While it may sound heretical, here is a radical thought: As an organization, you can do all the Bible study in the world, but without external results your little community and band of followers are a waste of effort in the kingdom of God. As efficacious as they may seem on the surface, these are simply internal efforts and expenses.

To understand the work that lies ahead of you, knowing what you as a community are good at, what most needs to be done where you are, and what those whom you will serve most value and need should then lead to everything else. The Corinthians appear to have lost touch—almost completely—with this concept, in the inward-directed turmoil and turbulence of their own local confusion. The logical target of this angst conveniently narrowed to the guy who loved them most and cared most about their lives and results. We are grateful that Paul understood this, and, despite his bruises and scars, labored on in this truly formidable management task.

TOOLBOX

The history of businesses and organizations is filled with stories of enterprises that have lost their way. In simple terms, they failed to *stick to business*. Although Paul does not use these modern terms in dealing with the Corinthian situation, the underlying structure of this approach shows up when the situation is analyzed.

- What is Paul's business?

- Much of Paul's task seems to be reminding his friends and followers what they should be spending their time on. Identify some of the ways Paul frames the business he is in.

8

Relationship Responsibility

Relationship is at the heart of organizational life. There are, however, numerous factors affecting the quality of the relationship of leader and follower. The closeness or depth of the relationship depends on many variables—personal responsibilities, commitment, age, experience, organizational culture and positional authority, much of which the leader may have little control over. At its core, however, leadership is a relationship of influence in which one person seeks to influence the behavior, attitudes, vision, values or beliefs of another.

In a relationship of influence everyone has some power, meaning each person chooses to stay in the relationship and to act in support of it. To make organizations not only effective but also places where individuals realize their own full potential, both leaders and followers have to be aligned over the long term with the same vision, values and objectives. Yet there are frequent situations where this is not the case.

Relying on the management and leadership principles of Paul, we observe some critical insights into one of the primary areas of failure for organizations—ineffective relationships. Exercising relationship responsibility is the key strategy in Paul's response to the situation in 2 Corinthians. In fact, the letter develops a concept of accountability between those in organizational relationships with broad and useful strokes.

Relationship responsibility can be unilateral, bilateral or multilateral. As leaders we obviously take responsibility for our organization, yet relationship responsibility for leaders and followers is unique in its claim to speak into another person's life.

Though bilateral relationships can be standard in partnerships and alliances, in full-blown leadership we hope for multilateral relational accountability. So-called 360 evaluations and similar tools have emerged to understand and assess multilateral behaviors in the personal and social skills of leaders and followers. The range of new articles and books on followers and followership also points to this important dynamic.

Unilateral Responsibility

However, there are times when leaders exercise unilateral responsibility. Paul recognizes that the situation he finds himself in is one where it is his responsibility alone to "right the ship" and to ensure that the problems are corrected. Such situations require cautious handling, since they are fraught with complications (as Paul's situation certainly shows). Attempting to offer advice or caution to an individual is difficult; to give direction and expect it to be carried out for sustained change in organizations creates an even thornier dilemma. In communities and organizations confusion inevitably arises when parties in a disagreement perceive this responsibility differently.

Relationship responsibility is similar to relationship management described by Daniel Goleman and Richard Boyatzis when writing about emotional and social intelligence. Relationship management refers to an individual's skill in using emotional intelligence when working with others, including resolving conflict, coaching and mentoring, influencing and inspiring, as well as handling teamwork issues.[1] Relationship management is where emotional intelligence becomes most visible to the people we deal with. The relationship management behaviors the authors identify impact the motivation and behaviors of others, and depend on our strengths in social awareness and self-management.

In 2 Corinthians Paul uses these skills as he approaches the people with his concerns. He is self-aware enough to recognize he must engage in conflict management and also wisely adds coaching and mentoring to the mix. Paul broadens his role as well, altering the relationship dynamic within the framework of responsibility for organizational results. In effect he "owns" the difficult place he finds himself.

Sometimes we take a different role in work relationships than we would in other settings. We may see ourselves as having little ability to effect responsible change or corporate results. This can make it easy to blame others for failures or disruptions, when in fact we have a more critical role to play. Results are dependent on everyone within the organization, and success demands the give-and-take of relationships. "To get any results," Drucker said, "requires from each member, independent responsibility and initiative."[2]

Places of Realized Potential

Places of realized potential may be possible only if individuals accept responsibility for their work, for their own lives and for their work relationships. "The condition of our hearts, the openness of our attitudes, the quality of our competence, the fidelity of our experience—these give vitality to the work experience and meaning to life."[3]

For all of us—leaders and followers—it is easy to slip into

dependency relationships, looking for others to solve our problems or to blame. With the ambiguities and complexities of the workplace, it is easy to abdicate responsibility to someone we think has answers. We live and work in the tension of a need for dependency and a desire for autonomy. Our dependent side wants to be cared for, wants someone to give us answers and to remove the risk of deciding. Our autonomous side wants control. The tension at the heart of the leadership relationship is about choosing to follow without abdicating responsibility for personal growth and decisions. Leadership that creates places where people flourish resists dependency and empowers followers to own responsibility for their choices and actions. The relationship of leadership in a flourishing organization involves empowering another to accept personal responsibility for life and work, and also to accept accountability for the results of the organization. Doing so can address some of our most existential needs as well as challenge us to reach our fullest potential.[4]

First Do No Harm

Relationship responsibility is a difficult idea for many followers, especially with the current rage for nonhierarchical organizations. Generally identified with the doctor's Hippocratic oath, the phrase "first do no harm" or "above all not knowingly do harm" was applied by Drucker to the concept of the professional in management. He reinterpreted the traditional phrase and saw it as representative of the idea that executives should exercise responsibility for the outcomes they create, whether planned or unplanned, whether direct or indirect. Drucker's concern that we do no harm reflects on the need for social responsibility and for a response by professional executives. However, he is also concerned with professionalism in the practice of management, and his overarching intent is for executives first to be personally responsible and to manage their own impacts. It is only after we address those concerns that we decide how our actions affect others.

Taking relationship responsibility involves a number of different action steps, some consciously made and having a direct effect on the others in the relationship, and some a byproduct of decisions that need to be made. In either case, those on the receiving end can find the leader—not just the leader's actions—offensive. In some situations this arises because the leader is required to express strong opinions or to tell others what to do, whether they like it or not, or whether or not they deny the leader the right to do so. While telling someone what to do should be the exception—and not every leader can exercise this type of authority—the extent to which a leader can and still be effective will depend on a number of factors, including a commitment to the business or mission of the company, and the ability of the leader (and followers) to exercise self-awareness, self-management, and emotional and social competencies.

This is one of the key issues for leaders. There is often, particularly in religious organizations, an implied duty to be nice, a duty that can supersede the requirement to accomplish the objectives of the organization. A senior administrator in a faith-based educational institution once told a female professor that the job of the faculty member was to "suckle" her students, implying that helping them to get through the course by supplying whatever they needed was the responsibility of the professor. (We're not sure how this applies to the male professors, however.)

Even where there is no direct line of authority or formal power, the task of owning responsibility for action, rather than being liked, is critical. Collins maintains that, rather than executive power, "legislative leadership," which requires persuasion, political currency and shared interest, is necessary to arrive at a right decision. But even in legislative leadership, being soft or nice or purely inclusive or consensus-building is not mandated. "It consists of making certain that the right decisions are made, no matter how difficult or painful, for the long-term good of the organization or the cause and the achievement of its mission. It exists independently of consensus or popularity." In fact, Collins identifies the suppression of candor as problematic, particularly in nonprofit institutions.[5]

DISRUPTIONS

Followers often expect those who have formal authority to lead in conflict and also to enforce norms, using these to reinforce and stabilize situations where there is disruption. The leader is expected to smooth things over and generally to help the group adjust their feelings when disruptions occur. But the leader is not expected to be the source of the disruption!

Exercising leadership has a critical role in reorienting us as leaders, making change happen and creating disequilibrium while also enabling us successfully to manage the turbulence and distress it generates. Ronald Heifetz and Donald Laurie claim that the difficult work of what they call "adaptive leadership" requires leaders to ask tough questions rather than provide solutions and to challenge the way things are done rather than simply maintain norms.[6] It is not that difficult for Paul to see the need to challenge the Corinthians' behaviors while passionately loving them. He wants them to change and adopt the behaviors and attitudes they were first taught, and he will not back down. As D. A. Carson notes,

Although Paul sees that in certain respects the evidence of his apostolic authority is the Corinthian church itself, along with other churches he has established, his authority is in no way dependent on those churches. If the Corinthian church should prove largely false, he feels free to destroy the work and remove the rot, in the hope of building something better. That is not his preference: he prefers to devote his energies to edification, not to discipline. But he is aware of the authority given to him to accomplish either task.[7]

Adaptive leadership requires leaders "to permit others to share ownership of problems—in effect, to take possession of a situation"[8] rather than becoming the object of criticism and unhappiness. This can cause discomfort to the point that followers will seek removal of the current leader. Social identity theory helps us understand why. It looks at group processes involved in the leadership/followership dynamic and examines how a sense of self is understood in terms of shared attributes that define group membership.[9]

As people identify strongly with a group, they look for the leader to exhibit a particular set of attributes—attitudes, behavior and customs—that have come to characterize the group and distinguish it from other groups. As membership evolves, the leader increasingly gains power to "define what the group stands for and what the social identity of its members is."[10] But this also means that the leader's identity, as a construction of group processes, is derived from the nature and standards of the group. If the leader gets out of step with the group by forcing too much change too quickly, she may find herself intensely criticized and eventually forced to back down or to exit.

In addition, as the group's power increases, it has been demonstrated that the perception of leadership effectiveness is more a product of groupthink than of true leadership qualities.[11] Followers look to the leader to represent them as the culture currently exists, whether or not the leader is actually effective at getting necessary results. This partially explains why ineffective leaders are tolerated longer than is good for the organization as a whole.

Culture change is always transformative, requiring a period of unlearning that can be psychologically painful. Among the characteristics required to manage this type of situation is a commitment to systemic thinking—underscoring that the world is complex, nonlinear and interconnected.[12] We know it is difficult to frame these ideas understandably when most people receive information as sound bites. And we all want to avoid distasteful information, as true as it may be. So we rarely speak of destroying culture when it is toxic or address the underlying causes of disruption, even in extreme situations where the strains placed on the organization and its leaders can potentially bring the leader or the organization down.

This does not mean that volatile situations must result in disaster. We find leaders weathering enormous challenges, though many are reluctant to acknowledge the firestorm they have lived through. When Robert Lane became CEO of Deere Company, he believed that the company was solid and offered a good product but fell short of being a great business. He approached this problem by first declaring that "every individual has inherent worth" but then deliberately claiming that Deere was "not a family," to reorient the employees' frame of reference. Although the company at one time "did have a family feel to it," Lane says, "I tell people that if you're not pulling your weight in a family, you're still invited to Thanksgiving dinner. But if you're not pulling your weight here, you're not part of the team."[13] These sound like harsh words, and many loudly criticized him for taking this approach. But the responsibility of the leader is to define reality. Without attention to the details of the business, the company would falter; Lane appropriately exercised relationship responsibility, holding others accountable in a way that no one else could.

How Much Is Enough?

What does it take to address these precarious situations? How much unilateral responsibility will be acceptable? Such issues are not easily handled, but to identify the organization whose culture has become stuck, Schein identifies three characteristics needed to unfreeze it:

- Enough *disconfirming data* to cause serious discomfort and disequilibrium.

- Connection of disconfirming data to important goals and ideals causing *anxiety and/or guilt.*

- Enough psychological safety: having enough sense of identity and integrity to go ahead with change.[14]

This does not mean that leaders expend energy in gathering negative data or inducing guilt. Nor does this condone harsh treatment, honesty at all cost or any other intentionally hurtful behavior. Rather it focuses the leader on ensuring transparent and ongoing communication, and constant attention to alignment with the business purpose or mission, especially with the meaningful Outside—the customer and external results— and the courage to take necessary but painful action.

Extensive studies establish that our capacity for empathy and for reading the feelings of others is one of the keys to successful work lives.[15] Empathy is not easy, nor does the process exempt the leader from feelings of pain or loss. De Pree asserts that "leaders don't inflict pain; they bear pain." Is he suggesting that leaders never make decisions that cause pain? Judging from examples where tough decisions occurred at Herman Miller, Inc., it does not appear so. Leaders experience and bear the realities of tough decisions and own them rather than blaming others or circumstances. To hold ourselves and others accountable is a major task of management.

De Pree reminds us that the other half of leadership is about learning. Developing a growth mindset toward intelligence—consciously recognizing that we can learn and improve, that effort makes a difference in our abilities, and that intelligence is not fixed—is important to personal development and how we perceive the mistakes of others. Stanford University psychologist Carol Dweck has done extensive work in this area. Hopefully we recognize that our maturation process requires experiencing painful consequences to our actions and learning to live with failure. Tom Peters writes often of how important setbacks and failures are to our learning and improvement. Making mistakes is part of how the brain optimally develops and protects us from other harm. Dweck's studies show that failure, when viewed as a learning experience—in other words, as an opportunity for self-improvement—can build and strengthen new neural pathways in the brain.[16]

As Drucker vividly reminds us, the one person to distrust is the one who does not make mistakes, who "never commits a blunder, never fails in what he tries to do. He is either a phony, or he stays with the safe, the tried, and the trivial."[17] In facing failure or in success, we must consider our relationship responsibilities, particularly in situations of directive action.

Paul and Relationship Responsibility

Paul's affection and love for this difficult little group in Corinth pervades the dialogue in 2 Corinthians, and we find that Paul truly cares for these deeply annoying people. He relates extensively to the emotions and hurts of those he has mentored and led. How does he stay connected and transparent with people who blame him, clearly have little respect for him and feel justified in criticizing him in public? Paul claims the right to challenge them by his role as founder and earlier apostolic validation, while the Corinthians continue to assert their independence and, not surprisingly, contest his right to act unilaterally. They do not want lectures or expressions of concern from Paul. They want to see demonstrations of spiritual power and the cultural trappings that accompany a successful leader, and they feel they have a right to demand these from him.

No doubt, from Paul's perspective, it helps that he believes he has been sent on a special mission planned by God to the congregation in Corinth in particular (2 Corinthians 1:1). He takes relationship responsibility first by explaining why he could not come on the trip as originally planned, offering his personal reasons and expressing his reaction to the hard feelings it caused. He tries to be as true to his word "as God is to his" (1:18), asserting that his failure to come was not out of indifference. What is he attempting to do? He wants to affirm his feelings for them, which have not changed, and to define the situation as he understands it. In particular, he knows they were counting on him to come and he intended to fulfill his promise—but perhaps not in the timeframe they envision. He presumes he caused them pain and harm by not coming and not keeping his commitment.

Why didn't he come? He writes that it was to spare them pain, "being considerate" of them, "not indifferent, not manipulative" (1:23). He knew if he came his visit would not be pleasant and he would end up disappointing them.

> That's why I decided not to make another visit that could only be painful to both of us. If by merely showing up I would put you in an embarrassingly painful position, how would you then be free to cheer and refresh me? That was my reason for writing a letter instead of coming—so I wouldn't have to spend a miserable time disappointing the very friends I had looked forward to cheering up. I was convinced at the time I wrote it that what was best for me was also best for you. As it turned out, there was pain enough just in writing that letter, more tears than ink on the parchment. But I didn't write it to cause pain; I wrote it so you would know how much I care—oh, more than care—love you! (2 Corinthians 2:1-4)

Like all good leaders, Paul is not just expressing his own feelings—being self-aware and self-managing in dealing with his direct relationship with these people—he is also teaching them how to respond to others, both by what he models and by his words. He is practicing relationship management in extending what he knows is important in such a way that others learn. For example, in chapter 2 he praises them for their actions in dealing with the "offender" in their group, noting, "The focus of my letter wasn't on punishing the offender but on getting you to take responsibility for the health of the church" (2:9). He focuses on relationship responsibility that requires them to act. Later in chapter 5, he credits God with the fresh start that we each get in life and that creates in us the ability to have right relationships with God and with others: "The old life is gone; a new life burgeons! Look at it! All this comes from the

God who settled the relationship between us and him, and then called us to settle our relationships with each other" (5:17-18).

Paul is not afraid to admit how much he cares about these people, even though they play havoc with his life and his ministry. The honesty of his communication with them is part of the message of God's love for them. It is not capable of being split between words and action. He is moved by Christ's love for them even when what he does or says seems to them to be not in their self-interest.

It is perhaps the underlying understanding (or lack of understanding) of power that most clearly influences the decision about how to lead in difficult circumstances. Paul's approach in 2 Corinthians reflects his eventual acceptance of his own powerlessness and reliance on God; indeed, it is the premise of the letter that he is not exercising personal power, even when he appears to act unilaterally. He is instead acting from a place of weakness and dependence on God.

Some leaders use words that sound similar, demonstrating personal sacrifice for the good of the followers or of the whole. Servant leadership is considered to embody these ideals. But we must be careful not to use language that doesn't square with the facts. Paul is able to talk about his utter weakness because he embodies it. Very few leaders are actually willing to replicate these things.

Paul's mission, like Jesus' before him, often meant challenging preconceived notions, calling attention to inconsistencies, examining actions in light of the truth of the gospel, and calling people to integrated and transformed minds, hearts and actions. Yet the very people confronted also recognized that he would lay down his life not only for them but also for those who accused him of being a religious fanatic or an egocentric charlatan.

Paul is concerned more with telling his readers *why* they

should respond to him, rather than *how* they should respond. Why? Because he has taken personal responsibility to be a person accountable to God and to survive the tough times, in part for their sake:

> We put no stumbling block in anyone's path, so that our ministry will not be discredited. Rather, as servants of God we commend ourselves in every way: . . . in hard work . . . in purity, understanding, patience and kindness; in the Holy Spirit and in sincere love; in truthful speech and in the power of God; with weapons of righteousness in the right hand and in the left. . . . We have wronged no one, we have corrupted no one, we have exploited no one. (2 Corinthians 6:3-7; 7:2 NIV)

Paul's intentions and motives are pure. That doesn't mean he's perfect or that there are not instances where he acts out of mixed motives. But he can genuinely say he only wants the best for them in terms of becoming Christ followers.

Paul goes on to say that he does these things even in the face of negative feedback and off-putting remarks and attitudes (6:8-9). He does it recognizing the complexity of emotions that come with being a leader (6:10) and being emotionally connected to them, even when they try to separate themselves (6:11-13). Paul is able to point to his own positive feelings and intentions for them, even if they don't mirror these. They may not like what he has done and they may revolt against his actions, but he can declare that he is not condemning them. In fact he still loves them, has confidence in them, takes pride in them, even is "greatly encouraged."

How can he do this? Perhaps because he focuses on the results of his actions toward them as the measurement of whether what he did was the right thing—he does not rely on their emotional response. It's not about him.

> Even if I caused you sorrow by my letter, I do not regret it. Though I did regret it—I see that my letter hurt you, but only for a little while— yet now I am happy, not because you were made sorry, but because your sorrow led you to repentance. For you became sorrowful as God intended and so were not harmed in any way by us. Godly sorrow brings repentance that leads to salvation and leaves no regret, but worldly sorrow brings death. See what this godly sorrow has produced in you: what earnestness, what eagerness to clear yourselves, what indignation, what alarm, what longing, what concern, what readiness to see justice done. At every point you have proved yourselves to be innocent in this matter. So even though I wrote to you, it was neither on account of the one who did the wrong nor on account of the injured party, but rather that before God you could see for yourselves how devoted to us you are. By all this we are encouraged. (2 Corinthians 7:8-13 NIV 1984)

His attention is focused on the results. What happened because of his behavior toward them and their response?

> When we arrived in Macedonia province, we couldn't settle down. The fights in the church and the fears in our hearts kept us on pins and needles. We couldn't relax because we didn't know how it would turn out. Then the God who lifts up the downcast lifted our heads and our hearts with the arrival of Titus. We were glad just to see him, but the true reassurance came in what he told us about you: how much you cared, how much you grieved, how concerned you were for me. I went from worry to tranquility in no time!

I know I distressed you greatly with my letter. Although I felt awful at the time, I don't feel at all bad now that I see how it turned out. The letter upset you, but only for a while. Now I'm glad—not that you were upset, but that you were jarred into turning things around. You let the distress bring you to God, not drive you from him. The result was all gain, no loss.

Distress that drives us to God does that. It turns us around. It gets us back in the way of salvation. We never regret that kind of pain. But those who let distress drive them away from God are full of regrets, end up on a deathbed of regrets.

And now, isn't it wonderful all the ways in which this distress has goaded you closer to God? You're more alive, more concerned, more sensitive, more reverent, more human, more passionate, more responsible. Looked at from any angle, you've come out of this with purity of heart. And that is what I was hoping for in the first place when I wrote the letter. My primary concern was not for the one who did the wrong or even the one wronged, but for you—that you would realize and act upon the deep, deep ties between us before God. That's what happened—and we felt just great. (2 Corinthians 7:5-13).

This passage reinforces Paul's attention to results, not to mollifying or appeasing those who are critical of him and his actions. He recognizes that his actions and the letter he sent distressed them, and he owns his own emotions of feeling badly—no doubt acknowledging failure as their leader. But he now sees the fruit of his actions—they were "jarred" into turning things around. He is satisfied that the tough challenges, the things that were clarified by his leadership behaviors, were used for their benefit because they allowed themselves to learn from this painful experience. This distressing chain of events drives them to God, just as it works for us; it "turns us around" and "gets us back in the way of salvation."

Like it did for Paul and eventually for the leaders in Corinth, a sense of personal powerlessness creates in us a renewed reliance on God and a willingness to listen to the Spirit so that we develop sensitivity to his voice and an awareness of when we are acting like we should. That is living in the truth, rather than being blinded by our own way of seeing and understanding. It is living in the light that shows us where we have failed and what we have taken on ourselves rather than entrusted to God.

In this instance, it appears that the group took what happened to them and decided how to embrace the pain and the differences and figure out their part in it. In the end, they did not sit back and continue to blame Paul or others but saw that they needed to change. They took relationship responsibility.

How did they change? What were the results? They were "more alive, more concerned, more sensitive, more reverent, more human, more passionate, more responsible" (7:11). They also developed a "purity of heart." Notice that the change is not only in actions but also in attitude and emotions. Sometimes change may take longer for one area than for another. Change in all aspects of our personality does not always occur simultaneously. But to be a follower of Christ, as Paul, means developing spiritual awareness, constantly monitoring how we live integrated lives. Paul hoped for this and held out for it. Arguably it took a lot of work (and prayer) on Paul's part with real angst operating in each party, but eventually they got to the point of managing their emotions and reactions, and accepted the truth about themselves and their situation.

Once again we see how the steps taken relationally are communicated down the line. Paul responded to their relationship with Titus—the person he was mentoring and working closely with:

> And then, when we saw how Titus felt—his exuberance over your response—our joy doubled. It was wonderful to see how revived and refreshed he was by everything you did. If I went out on a limb in telling Titus how great I thought you were, you didn't cut off that limb. As it turned out, I hadn't exaggerated one bit. Titus saw for himself that everything I had said about you was true. He can't quit talking about it, going over again and again the story of your prompt obedience, and the dignity and sensitivity of your hospitality. He was quite overwhelmed by it all! And I couldn't be more pleased—I'm so confident and proud of you. (2 Corinthians 7:13-16)

We see that what Paul is celebrating once more is the result—their prompt obedience and the manner in which they hosted Titus.

Later, in chapters 10–13 Paul has a different mindset. As Carson notes, "There is a time for subtle dealings; there is also a time for blunt confrontation. As a wise counselor, Paul knows the difference."[18] Earlier, though, when building his case against the super-apostles Paul is essentially gentle with his words, even if a little sarcastic and ironic at times. He wants the Corinthian Christians to think seriously about the type of leaders the super-apostles are, and how to judge between those worth emulating and those not. In the last three chapters of the book he looks in detail at their failings and faults them for allowing the interlopers to gain a foothold in the Corinthian church. They have a mess on their hands for sure, but it is a mess of their own making.

A Final Thought: Relationship Responsibility

One leader survived battering by a boss and lived to tell what she learned:

> I learned that if I had to, I would do the same thing all over again, stand up against any leader behaving in an abusive manner, whether directed toward myself or a co-worker.
>
> I learned that this type of hurt from an abusive Christian leader hurts at many levels: as a friend, as someone you trusted, as someone representing the church, as someone who was my pastor and betrayed me and those he seemed to care about.
>
> I learned what it means to let go when it is not healthy even when that means you are alone.
>
> I learned disengaging did not mean I was giving up.
>
> I learned that you need to surround yourself with people who share your values and speak truth to you and support you through the refining fire . . . and that what is left after you let go of the bad stuff is REALLY good and the people who stand by you are really quality people that you are proud to call your friends.
>
> I experienced what it is to suffer for my values and to have to trust myself and what God was telling me despite what others were saying—even in the church.
>
> I learned that maybe why God was allowing suffering was that he trusted me, that He wanted to use my suffering and circumstances for plans and purposes that were bigger than mine.

I learned that standing up for what you believe in COSTS you, not just once but in many waves, over time. You need to prepare yourself for the long haul and be emotionally resilient.

I learned that "hurt people, hurt people" and that wounded leaders who don't heal their woundedness, spill it on to others.

I learned that the more I let go and let God work, the more I learned.

TOOLBOX

When faced with competition for the top leadership position after building an organization from scratch, or when the project or organization she has given her life to is threatened with destruction, what is the leader's response?

In Paul's case he is willing to take whatever measures will work to save it, unafraid of third parties but accountable to God. He is kind and severe, humble and dictatorial—as perhaps fits his background, personality and situation. What are the measures Paul undertakes in exercising relationship responsibility with the Corinthians?

Hope, Generosity and Power

Paul's second letter to the Corinthians abounds with recovery strategies—methods for tackling both the issues that create battering (introduced in chapter six, "The Management of Sin"), and the emotional and psychological responses to such behaviors. It is a great strength of this letter; perhaps the central message to battered leaders is one of hope for the future through continuing to work at managing the relationship with followers. As noted earlier, the first task of the leader is to define reality for the organization; this forms the crux of Paul's strategy as the apostle unfolds a complex process of reframing for the Corinthians. Some of the themes Paul emphasizes include:

- Taking personal responsibility
- Gaining knowledge
- Managing up
- Being hopeful
- Staying generous
- Letting God empower you

Of all the strategies implemented by Paul, none stands out like letting God empower you. It is really the critical message of 2 Corinthians. Paul recognized that nothing he had done or could do would matter if God was not the force behind it.

Where we start determines what we see. As a runner for most of her adult life, Janis appreciates that your perception of a certain route can change dramatically when you run it backwards. It completely changes how you understand the path, even what you see. What you absorb when the familiar terrain becomes unfamiliar is striking.

So too with our minds and hearts. When we are open to new discoveries and are willing to face up to the way our brains are wired, only then can we begin to reframe our experiences. This begins with an awareness of beliefs and assumptions. Margaret Wheatley reflects, "My true self is aware of what I am doing and why I am doing it, while participating in the moment, and then reorienting my responses."[1]

Reorienting by beginning at a different place can help initiate not only a belief but also an expectancy. Negative experiences are not the whole story; there is another perspective and a different mindset that can eventually be discerned. Beginning here creates a stronger likelihood that we will sort out the experience eventually. The markers along the path that we revisit and the voices now being replayed will take on new and distinct meanings. This chapter looks at ways we can bring these situations into new focus and reorient ourselves to see people and situations through new lenses.

REORIENTING

Getting a first set of eyeglasses can be a dizzying experience. We may think our vision isn't any better until our eyes adjust and we become comfortable wearing them. So too with being battered. Finding new ways to understand our experiences can be difficult; eventually we find that the new clarity is preferred and offers a greater opportunity for true healing.

Too often we sweep issues under the carpet, ignore them or act nice, when inside we are dying. The challenge is to manage the issues that create destructive places, that move away from places of realized potential. There are psychologists and counselors, self-help books and online resources to address these types of concerns. But for those who value the lessons of Paul there is an amazing amount to learn from his experience. What follows is a set of instructions for leaders to survive toxic situations as well as to find personal health and productivity in the aftermath of battering.

The practices we propose are aligned with the practices Paul espouses and models. How we work them out in our lives is up to us!

Taking Personal Responsibility

Taking responsibility means understanding ourselves and the role we play in creating our own drama. We used to tell one of our children who really enjoyed creating emotional drama, "Don't be a victim." By this we meant there were actions she could take to make her life and her reactions to events more productive. The key to beginning such a process, however, is to see reality[2] and recognize our own culpability. We must recognize our own mistakes and failures and take steps to address them. "In the end, it is important to remember that we cannot become what we need to be by remaining what we are."[3]

Sometimes, of course, it's impossible on our own—there are psychological, genetic or social factors that restrict our ability to respond positively to these experiences of self. But frequently as battered leaders we have access to personal or organizational tools and practices to help us confront and then be proactive about our responses to being battered. These include the exercise of emotional and social competencies, prayer, meditation and mindfulness, and tools for self-management. (Many of these, often pivotal for beginning the recovery process, are covered in chapter six, "The Management of Sin.")

You have to own your role in leading change to make things better. This is a major source of conflict, discomfort and possibly added opportunity for becoming battered. The course it is played out on is more like a miniature golf course than it is like a racetrack. There are complexities, hidden traps, surprising twists and more challenges than first appear; it is not clearly laid out. According to Heifetz the complexity of change makes leadership "dangerous":

> Sure, you have to protect people from change. But you also have to "unprotect" them. It's dangerous to challenge people in a way that will require changes in their priorities, their values, their habits. It's dangerous to try to persuade people to take more responsibility than they feel comfortable with. And that's why so many leaders get marginalized, diverted, attacked, seduced.[4]

The strategy required is that we figure out how to stir the pot without letting it boil over, regulate the disequilibrium and strive to keep people in a productive discomfort zone. As a leader, you need to be mindful of how you are using your power in these types of situations.

Paradoxically, it may be best for us to push ourselves into discomfort zones to expand our ability to thrash around and come out of situations bruised but intact. Too often we live where we are most comfortable rather than in the swirling reality of our complex world.

Where conflict surfaces or situations create hardship or discouragement, a leader has to evaluate. As Jim Collins notes in *Good to Great*, leaders of great companies look in the mirror to assign blame and look out their window at the company to assign credit. So taking blame is not necessarily a bad thing. But one of the first sensations to surface for many people in evaluating their responsibility for conflict situations and emotional hardship is that of failure. If it doesn't then you may need to look at whether you are too narcissistic or whether you have ever really had to confront actual failure. To do so is a difficult thing.

Most people experienced in management and leadership value conflict. Heifetz calls it the primary engine of creativity and innovation.

> Companies tend to be allergic to conflict—particularly companies that have been in operation for a long time. Being averse to conflict is understandable. Conflict is dangerous: It can damage relationships. It can threaten friendships. But conflict is the primary engine of creativity and innovation. People don't learn by staring into a mirror; people learn by encountering difference. So hand in hand with the courage to face reality comes the courage to surface and orchestrate conflicts.[5]

Leaders of the future need to have the stomach for conflict and uncertainty—among their people and within themselves.

GAINING KNOWLEDGE

It is amazing how many religious or spiritual people are afraid of knowledge. They see a conspiracy behind every thought that does not fit their worldview or that does not conform to their concept of how things are or what they believe, in the most common use of the term. In contrast some Christ followers have chosen to adopt the concept that "all truth is God's truth," opening the door to appreciate new knowledge and gain insight.

One pastor we know was very much a self-starter and learner. He saw little value in structured learning in a classroom. Because he was able to integrate book knowledge by himself, he did not see any reason to enroll in a formal program and get an advanced degree. "What is the value of engaging in a classroom setting?" he asked. The answer that came to mind

> "You groped your way through that murk once, but no longer. You're out in the open now. The bright light of Christ makes your way plain. So no more stumbling around. Get on with it! The good, the right, the true— these are the actions appropriate for daylight hours. Figure out what will please Christ, and then do it."
> (Ephesians 5:8-10)

for Janis was the very act of engaging "live" with others. When people are self-learners, they have the time to construct arguments leisurely and only respond with their own counterbalance. This can lead to a myopic perspective on the subject matter. Especially for a leader whose responsibilities include constantly communicating with others, the most valued experience can be the forced interaction. In the right kind of classroom you cannot sit idly by and let your ideas be internalized. Instead you should have to defend them; you should need to be quick to spot deficiencies in your argument as well as in the arguments being pressed by someone else. This ability is cultivated in the classroom, as well as in other settings where power distance is minimized.

So too, in the workplace we encounter the issue of individuals who are not able to constructively engage with issues or new ideas. Perhaps they have not been in an environment where they are held accountable for the promotion of ideas and the practices those ideas envision. In addition, we may find that their views are anchored in other emotional matters and that if we listen closely we can learn something more about them and about our reactions to them. When people in a group—whether it be a classroom, a team meeting or a weekly update session—begin to haggle over an issue, we learn a lot. As Heifetz points out, "There's an enormous amount of information in the haggling, and that information tells us quite a lot about the values, the history, and the personal stakes that people bring to an argument."[6]

MANAGING UP

Surely you have noticed that sometimes you can copy things from an Acrobat PDF file, and sometimes you can't. The provider has generally been intentional in deciding what you can and cannot copy. There's an underlying policy at work that protects the creator's property, but only rarely is it actually stated.

The same thing is true for some leaders. They too have underlying policies or processes at work—although they are not called that—which only allow them to engage on certain issues (sometimes none at all). We can get only "so close" to them, and no closer. Occasionally they tell us what those boundaries are, but some don't even know what they are. Mostly we have to guess, and if we guess wrongly it can mean the end of a job or the end of a relationship, or sometimes both.

As a person struggling within an organization and with the leadership of it, you may be the target of negative attention from the formal leadership because in fact you are leading, but without formalized power or authority. Heifetz observes that "grassroots leaders often generate 'sticky' attention—attention that sticks to them personally, rather than to their agenda. To use a different metaphor, it's never comfortable to be a lightning rod. The easiest way for an organization to neutralize the disturbance that you represent is to neutralize you."[7]

What should you do? While many of us love to spend time beside the water cooler or on our social networking site criticizing the boss, there will be little to show for such efforts. Instead Dee Hock, in his classic article on chaordic leadership, describes the need for significant attention to "managing up."[8] Drucker also emphasizes learning how the leader works and using that knowledge to increase both your and your boss's results. Looking at the leader as a person and seeking to understand his point of view, the pressures he is working under and the context for his actions may be more beneficial in the long run. "Most bosses are already operating near the limit of how much distress they can tolerate—of how much disequilibrium, confusion, and chaos they can stomach. Naturally, they're inclined to suppress additional disturbances."[9] In the end, if we each understand how we contribute to the situation, we may be able to better understand the situation and adapt new strategies.

We may have to narrow our options: either vocally criticize the boss, leave the organization or the unit, or positively try to change the situation. For many, this is a critical juncture; looking at the roles of exit, voice and loyalty offers a way to frame our options.

EXITING WELL

In terms of recovery strategies, the first decision many of us have to make is whether to exercise voice or exit (or both), and then to understand how we came to that decision. By understanding the relationship between exit and voice, and the interplay that loyalty has with these choices, we may also, as organizational agents, be better able to address concerns and creatively improve the organizational culture.

It requires thinking about the choices we have. Albert Hirschman's work on exit and voice, though offered from an economic perspective, can be useful in reflecting on our options.[10] Members of any organization—whether a business, a volunteer group or a nation—have essentially two possible responses when they feel the organization is no longer providing a benefit. They can exit, withdraw from the relationship, or exercise voice. Voice involves an attempt to repair or improve the relationship by expressing themselves either through a complaint process or by offering suggestions for change. Examples include unhappy customers or employees who express their complaints to the manager versus those who take their business or know-how elsewhere. When we think about these options, however, it is clear that some people do both. What affects this decision is the third variable, which Hirschman labels loyalty; in general it neutralizes the tendency to exit.

When someone exercises the option to exit they may do so quietly or loudly. Some occasions are confrontational and others are innocuous. In general, exercising voice means that you are attempting to help the organization by expressing the reason for your concerns. Exit can be reduced by the opportunity to express feedback or criticism; however, where members are not given the opportunity to express their opinion or to offer a dissenting view, there may be no other option but to exit. Thus, some organizations or departments become nothing more than revolving doors.

The interplay of loyalty affects how and to what extent we exercise exit or voice. Where there is loyalty to the organization we may not be so anxious to exit, especially where our options upon exiting are not so appealing (e.g., a tight job market or financial hurdles to relocating). Hirschman notes that in choosing between voice and exit, the tendency is for voice to lose out "not necessarily because it would be less effective than exit, but because its effectiveness depends on the *discovery* of *new* ways of exerting influence and pressure toward recovery."[11] He explains that loyalty "helps to redress the balance by raising the cost of exit" and thus pushes people into the "alternative, creativity-requiring course of action from which they would normally recoil."[12]

Obviously, there are some people who exit for other reasons. As strange as it may seem, some people simply cannot handle success. They fear they will be found to be charlatans or frauds. Though they achieved results, they want to escape before they are "found out." Others leave because they need to find a new challenge. Some people will create situations of stress just to generate a situation where the consequence requires them to leave. We have all seen very successful leaders step down to go to a new position or a totally different endeavor for no apparent reason—sometimes they will say it was money or position although there appears to be little difference.

It is often difficult to know at the time whether we have made the right decision or not. It is typically only in hindsight that it is made clear, and it is at that point that we recognize that it took something more than our own resilience or stupidity (depending on your personal viewpoint) to make a bad situation have a positive result. One leader describes the result of his decision to stay in the midst of a very unhealthy structure:

If you'd have asked me at that point to measure the results of this God, Spirit-led decision, I would have said disastrous. . . . [T]his one . . . looked like a spectacular failure. But it didn't turn out that way. It turned out to be exactly what was needed. Somebody needed to hunker down and survive this pathological problem that had existed from the founding of the school and it was my being there that enabled us to weed it out of the system and get a healthy board and a healthy faculty and everything in place. So along from this perspective, I can say, "Yeah, very good results."

BEING HOPEFUL

Not many of us could have endured what Paul did and still have the sense of hope and resilience that we find in 2 Corinthians. We must remind ourselves that movement is happening independently of us. After the fact we usually discover, through a maze of circumstances and interaction with networks, that God has always been active. Seeing ourselves and our purposes (mission) in conjunction with other activity where God is at work can provide reassurance when things get difficult.

Earlier we mentioned the need to handle and learn from failure.

> "If the Government of Condemnation was impressive, how about this Government of Affirmation? Bright as that old government was, it would look downright dull alongside this new one. If that makeshift arrangement impressed us, how much more this brightly shining government installed for eternity? With that kind of hope to excite us, nothing holds us back."
> (2 Corinthians 3:9-12)

We now know that one of the major differences between those who fail and those who succeed is that those who remain hopeful succeed. They do not see the failure as the "end all" of their lives. It is one experience—hopefully one from which they learn. There are parts of Jack Welch's management philosophy we would disagree with, but in telling us how important it is for managers to "get back up on the horse," he offers important advice:

> We look for people that are not perfect. People that have made mistakes, but know how to quickly get back up on the horse when they've been thrown off, and those that turn the loss around into a win. It isn't about never making mistakes; it's about getting back up and moving forward toward the results. If someone has never experienced falling off and shown their ability to get back up, they might not be the managers we want.[13]

De Pree characterizes hope as "a functional force" that creates choices; hope is part of what a leader owes to others in the organization. Choice is always directly connected to hope. So too is success. As De Pree explains it, if a person cannot succeed they cannot have hope, "and if they can't have hope, it's going to be, at best, a very ordinary organization."[14]

In *Good to Great*, Jim Collins interviewed James Stockdale, the highest ranking United States military officer in the "Hanoi Hilton" prisoner-of-war camp during the Vietnam conflict. Although brutally tortured during his eight-year incarceration, he came away struck by how some men were able to tolerate their inhuman conditions better than others. He found that it hinged, in part, on this: "You must never confuse faith that you will prevail in the end—which you can never afford to lose—with the discipline to confront the most brutal facts of your current reality, whatever they may be"[15]—words that the apostle Paul could have written.

Likewise, Mihaly Csikszentmihalyi discovered that among thirty-nine visionary business leaders chosen by their peers as combining high achievement with strong moral commitment, one of the traits shared by all was optimism.[16] They believed not only in their ability to solve problems but also in the fundamental trustworthiness and decency of the people they dealt with.

CONTEMPLATING HOPE

Paul uses a number of different metaphors, including buildings, shacks, tents, houses, spacious living conditions, true home and homecoming. These terms offer us new perspectives when we contemplate hope.

> God of all healing counsel! He comes alongside us when we go through hard times, and before you know it, he brings us alongside someone else who is going through hard times so that we can be there for that person just as God was there for us.
>
> When we suffer for Jesus, it works out for your healing and salvation. If we are treated well, given a helping hand and encouraging word, that also works to your benefit, spurring you on, face forward, unflinching. Your hard times are also our hard times. When we see that you're just as willing to endure the hard times as to enjoy the good times, we know you're going to make it, no doubt about it. (2 Corinthians 1:3-7)

We have moved often, and each home has its own unique personality and quirks. Each required adjustments to make it a family home. When Janis asked the kids once which home they liked the best, they all said the one we occupied before the middle child went off to college. Why? Because it was a fixer-upper and they felt the transformation was a great model of turning something old and ugly into something welcoming and gracious.

We were quite surprised! What we remembered were the turquoise appliances, the one small window-unit air conditioner battling the 110 degrees outside, the hard work and elbow grease that went into remodeling it—using a jackhammer to get up the tile—and pulling off the ugly wallpaper on wall after wall. We realized that transformation is awe-inspiring; it catches our imagination and provides us fuel for other opportunities for growth and change, preparing us for the next level of the challenges ahead.

Staying Open and Generous

Frequently we feel battered because we believe we failed to live up to our own or other's expectations—that we let people down. Tied to this is a sense of disappointment with how we did not meet our potential or use our resources wisely. In many cases, there is no one else to blame, and the attitudes and expressions of disappointment of others contribute to our weakened emotional state.

When we are hurting and depressed or despondent, the first thing we want to do is withdraw. We want to stay away from the people we used to surround ourselves with—partially because we are ashamed or embarrassed, but also because we do not want to have the wound continually irritated or reopened. We cannot handle the banter, the questions or, worst of all, the sympathy. We may also feel insecure about our futures, our possibilities for other employment, our ability to regain a steady income or our sense of control over our lives. So what do we do? We keep to ourselves—not only in terms of people but in terms of time, energy and attention. We focus inwardly and on our own situation. While this is okay for a time, we often continue at this long after we should.

We need to remind ourselves to reach out in every way—in who we are and what we mean to people personally. Many of these people were not involved in our demise but will feel that they are being blamed.

If we hold anything back from God, it's very hard to be generous. If we really trust God, its easy to be generous. If we live in fear we won't have enough, then we can't really give it away to others—whether it's money, love, time or even trust. Openness, along with the dimension of staying hopeful, is a good indicator of our spiritual health.

Some leaders are able to recognize this. In describing how his own spiritual health is "absolutely critical" to how he responds to people, one leader adopts methods for confronting his challenges. He has adopted the H.A.L.T. method from Alcoholics Anonymous, which he uses at least monthly and sometimes daily:

> The question you ask yourself, is the mantra—never get too hungry, too angry, too lonely. In my personal times . . . I'll evaluate myself based on that. Where am I too isolated? Am I too tired? If so is it a physical tired? Is it a spiritual tired? What is making me tired? I try to really evaluate—personally make sure that I'm trying to fire all the cylinders in that environment.

Other factors that appear to be critical to survival or recovery are sometimes considered spiritual virtues as well, such as humility, empathy or compassion.

Being generous with our resources is another way to confront our pain. Paul's discussion of the offering for the Macedonians and the perhaps unintentional lesson in fundraising offers us an additional perspective on giving that reinforces this lesson in beautiful ways.

As a battered leader, Paul doesn't take anything for granted. He sees the drift among the Corinthians toward the meaningless Inside and its negative impact on their focus. He knows what they need to see and hear to get back on track. But more than that, he knows that they need to have their eyes directed back toward the meaningful Outside. He can lead them, but they also bear responsibility for their own commitment to the Corinthian business.

> Test yourselves to make sure you are solid in the faith. Don't drift along taking everything for granted. Give yourselves regular checkups. You need firsthand evidence, not mere hearsay, that Jesus Christ is in you. Test it out. If you fail the test, do something about it. (2 Corinthians 13:5)

TOOLBOX

Here is one person's story of recovery and how positive results came from her interaction in a stressful leadership situation.

> I work on a team led by a woman who is an accepting, warm, introverted artistic writer. She has never met a person she doesn't like and sees the good in all. I am an analytical, quality control, external processor that can always imagine a new approach. I like things organized and well planned out as much ahead of time as possible. We have worked together for 30 years. Often we have

worked at opposite ends of the same organization. We have tried to work closer because we love and admire each other, but our approaches are extremely different and we can create a fair amount of frustration and anxiety for each other.

Recently we were assigned a project together. We believe we were assigned not only to do this project, but also to do it jointly by God. Otherwise, between us we could have come up with a way to do it together, separately. My dear kind friend was to lead it. While she has many outstanding leadership qualities, she is happy not to lead; I am happy to lead.

There was no end to my second-guessing. I thought of each detail I would have approached differently. Being an external processor, I'm afraid to say she heard most of those thoughts. I could tell I was wearing her down; she could tell she was wearing me down. We prayed together, we relied on our years of commitment to each other, and we deferred through clenched teeth and tears. We just kept moving, and we did make progress, but the cost was high to us both. We each secretly thought about quitting. Well, she thought more secretly than I.

One night I had a dream. It was simple—an imposing man kindly but firmly told me, "Stop resisting your friend." He used her name, but we'll call her my friend. I woke up knowing that God was instructing me. I hadn't really thought of it as resisting; I was just trying to get the job done the "best" way. It was mostly about an attitude of my heart. I could see the difference. The loaded words, the irritation, the "what's wrong with you anyway?" created pain for us both, and lots of wasted energy.

So I tried it. What I had been doing was like riding on top of a stagecoach beside the driver. Although the driver had the reins in hand, I kept jumping onto the horses and steering them around the corners. This caused my friend, the driver's reigns to go slack and useless.

I asked for God's help because I knew I needed His help as I made every effort to restrain this attitude of "I have a better way to do that." It worked. What worked was a gradual decrease in frustration and trust re-entered our relationship. This wasn't magic, we spent a fair share of time with her look of frustration and my realization I had done it again—not just adding my contribution, but resisting her.

We are gradually settling into a new system. The fact that we are entering our third and last year on the project is its own success, and a show of God at work in His people. I'm grateful for His instruction through a dream.

Write your own story of a situation where you have found positive impacts from what could have been a disaster.

Letting God

In the last few chapters we discussed several recovery strategies, steps that can put us on the path to healing. We discuss the last one, letting God empower us, in this concluding chapter. Of all the strategies implemented by Paul, none stands out like this one. It is really the critical message of 2 Corinthians. Paul recognizes that nothing he has done or could do would matter if God was not the force behind it.

PAUL, AUTHORITY AND THE KINGDOM OF GOD

As hard as he fought for and loved the individuals who made up the church in Corinth, Paul understood that the church is really not the last and best hope of people who call themselves Christ followers—the kingdom of God is.

The kingdom challenges us with understanding both the now and the not-yet. We can tolerate the now, perhaps sinfully tainted by fellow Christians claiming the authority of the church, because of the not-yet promise of the kingdom. The Corinthian church challenged Paul by unilaterally withdrawing from him the right to be its leader. Paul stands, with apostolic authority, in the not-yet of the kingdom and says, "But you are wrong and here's why."

If you're a battered leader in a so-called Christian organization (and, remember, if you are not battered, you have not really led), the answer seems simple—just stand on your "apostolic" authority in the kingdom and tell those intransigent followers who are beating you up that you are the boss. But this is a use of power that will not work in the not-yet (and does not generally work very well in the here and now!). It may sound like this is what Paul is doing, but kingdom theology has finer shades of meaning.

In fact, Paul seems to be defusing and reframing the entire context of power in Corinth. Even his defensiveness about refusing to take their money effectively removes money as a source of power from the dialogue. And remember, Paul's power differential appears to be at zero; this is true leadership and the right foundation to create a different understanding of power.

> You who have been demanding proof that Christ speaks through me will get more than you bargained for. You'll get the full force of Christ, don't think you won't. He was sheer weakness and humiliation when he was killed on the cross, but oh, he's alive now—in the mighty power of God! We weren't much to look at, either, when we were humiliated among you, but when we deal with you this next time, we'll be alive in Christ, strengthened by God. (2 Corinthians 13:3-4)

The power used here flows out of weakness and humiliation. It is grounded in the ultimate reality and deepest humiliation of a naked man/God tortured and bleeding on a cross. It is truly "leading without power." Though Paul clearly envisions results in the *now*, that is, the next time he shows up in Corinth, sometimes we have to understand that resolution of the issue is actually taking place in the *not-yet*. We do not really know what happened when Paul arrived, and in the end, it is not as important as understanding the complexities of kingdom authority and results.

It is important to recognize that Paul's authority is that of both founder and apostle. Part of Paul's appeal for obedience flows from his role as "father" of this particular community. In the Corinthian case the dialogue gets parental at times, with undertones of raising an adolescent. (Those of you who have been there will know immediately what we are talking about.) And if being founder was not enough, Paul claims further to be an apostle, founder not only of the Corinthian church but also, with the Twelve, cofounder of the whole community of Jesus. Paul repeatedly calls attention to the place of high visibility from which he speaks: "We stand in Christ's presence when we speak; God looks us in the face. We get what we say straight from God and say it as honestly as we can" (2 Corinthians 2:17). This is unique positioning and buttresses Paul's authority as founder, apostle and member of the inner circle. It is reminiscent of Jesus in John 14, claiming to do only what he sees the Father doing. It is special authority and not necessarily available to the rest of us. It highlights the problem of simplistic application of organizational situations in Scripture to all of life. We have to be careful and wise in how we use the Bible. At the same time, always looking to the Father as we live and act is of benefit. It is a permanent posture of inclining our ears—almost a physical orientation of nonstop listening, a variation on praying without ceasing, an outward and visible appearance of humility (and not the false kind!).

Our limited understanding of time in the not-yet also confuses us. The key to the not-yet is that it has nothing to do with today, next week or last year. It simply exists completely outside this paradigm and system. We really have no tools to understand this, which is why it gets so arcane. It is one of those faith issues that we are challenged by when we become Christ followers. It is a mystery, but we gain some wisdom when we compare two understandings of time: *chronos* and *kairos*. The former is indicated on my wristwatch and the latter invades our existence when God wills it. You can tell the difference.

It is easier for a follower of Jesus to understand this because faith is the vehicle that breaks through the closed systems of this world, and time is one of those more perplexing systems. George Eldon Ladd handled this well in *The Presence of the Future.*[1] So we will not necessarily see the results we want in the now. This does not mean, however, that there are not results.

> We don't want you in the dark, friends, about how hard it was when all this came down on us in Asia province. It was so bad we didn't think we were going to make it. We felt like we'd been sent to death row, that it was all over for us. As it turned out, it was the best thing that could have happened. Instead of trusting in our own strength or wits to get out of it, we were forced to trust God totally—not a bad idea since he's the God who raises the dead! And he did it, rescued us from certain doom. And he'll do it again, rescuing us as many times as we need rescuing. (2 Corinthians 1:8-10)

A FEW CONCLUDING THOUGHTS

We first conceived of this book in June 2006. As we have listened to people, felt their hurt and shared our stories, it became clear that there were painful but commonly experienced situations that needed to be shared openly. While we realized to some degree that the subject would not be popular and that it would entail some careful editing of events and people, we were not ready for how much our own lives would be affected. As we wrote, talked, listened, and tied events and concepts together, we had to relive with others many past pain-filled experiences; this is not something most of us enjoy doing. In wrapping up this book, we hope we are also wrapping up a lot of pain, for ourselves and others, both from being battered over the years as well as brand-new wounds.

It is interesting that many fresh wounds have been received since we started this journey—some even from people who were part of the process of studying 2 Corinthians with us, sharing ideas and their personal experiences. We keep telling ourselves that it happened so that we would have fresh fodder for the book! While the fresh and open wounds have been hurtful, they remind us that each new painful event, whether involving institutions or individuals, reinforces the lessons of Paul from 2 Corinthians. Some days we felt like we could say with him that we felt "beaten within an inch of our lives" (6:9). While not physically flogged and thrashed as he was, we have definitely been crushed. Yet we, with Paul, also want to say, "We don't just put up with our limitations; we celebrate them, and then go on to celebrate every strength, every triumph of the truth in [us]" (13:9).

Recovery may lie not only in perspective but also in timing. Most of us who have been battered know that time does not heal all wounds. On the other hand, we know that over time many of the wounds close over and the scar tissue is not so obvious. We can also recognize, after the fact, how even the difficult and painful circumstances in our lives, whether administered by broken individuals or toxic systems, have ultimately resulted in amazingly wonderful and new opportunities, relationships and learning. But it requires that we focus on God and not on the obstacle—whether the person or the sin. When we focus there we feel despair, but when we focus on the power of God we see that ultimate control rests there.

Like the message of Paul, the central message of this book is meant to be one of hope and confidence in God. If we had not found the message of Paul to be as applicable as it is, we may not have been able to write it! We hope you find it encouraging and healing as well.

Appendix

The Corinthian Christians gave their founding pastor, Paul, more trouble than all his other churches put together. No sooner did Paul get one problem straightened out in Corinth than three more appeared. . . .

The provocation for Paul's second letter to the Christians in Corinth was an attack on his leadership. In his first letter, though he wrote most kindly and sympathetically, he didn't mince words. He wrote with the confident authority of a pastor who understands the ways God's salvation works and the kind of community that comes into being as a result. At least some of what he wrote to them was hard to hear and hard to take.

So they bucked his authority—accused him of inconsistencies, impugned his motives, questioned his credentials. They didn't argue with what he had written; they simply denied his right to tell them what to do. . . .

Because leadership is necessarily an exercise of authority, it easily shifts into an exercise of power. But the minute it does that, it begins to inflict damage on both the leader and the led. Paul, studying Jesus, had learned a kind of leadership in which he managed to stay out of the way so that the others could deal with God without having to go through him. All who are called to exercise leadership in whatever capacity—parent or coach, pastor or president, teacher or manager—can be grateful to Paul for this letter, and to the Corinthians for provoking it.

Eugene Peterson, introduction to 2 Corinthians, *The Message*

Notes

Chapter 1: If You Haven't Bled, You Haven't Led

[1]We will develop the term *battered* as the book unfolds. In general, if you have been, you probably know it. More specifically, the numerous lists that Paul supplies throughout 2 Corinthians form a sound foundation. By the end of the book, any sincere and self-aware leader should be able to identify her own unique set of battering circumstances.

[2]E. Peterson, introduction to 2 Corinthians, *The Message: The New Testament in Contemporary Language* (Colorado Springs: NavPress, 1993), p. 368.

[3]Ibid.

[4]Adapted from B. P. Shapiro, *An Introduction to Cases* (Cambridge, Mass.: Harvard Business School Publishing, 1988).

[5]T. Barnett, "Management Functions," in *Reference for Business: Encyclopedia of Business*, 2nd ed. (n.d.), retrieved November 29, 2010, www.referencefor business.com/management/Log-Mar/Management-Functions.html.

[6]J. Collins, *Good to Great and the Social Sectors* (New York: HarperCollins, 2005), pp. 11-13.

[7]D. Goleman, *Emotional Intelligence* (New York: Bantam Books, 1995).

Chapter 2: The Leadership Conundrum

[1]E. Peterson, introduction to 2 Corinthians, *The Message: The New Testament in Contemporary Language* (Colorado Springs: NavPress, 1993), p. 368.

[2]When some leaders get battered, the cause can often be found in the actions of other leaders, sometimes senior leaders, who have become toxic. A battered leader ends up in the middle when this toxic leader influences the battered leader's followers. We call this a "toxic triangle." We cover this later when discussing *triangulation*.

[3]J. Lipman-Blumen, "Toxic Leadership in Times of Crisis: The Creation of God" (paper presented at 5th Henry Luce Leadership Conference, Marietta Ohio, October 12, 2001), p. 4.

[4]In the sixteenth century, Puritan factions in the Church of England "wearied" out traditional Anglican ministers by subtly (and not so subtly) harassing them until they resigned their positions.

[5]C. D. Bultena and R. B. Whatcott, "Bushwacked at Work: A Comparative Analysis of Mobbing and Bullying at Work," *Proceedings of ASBBS* 15, no. 1 (2008): 652-66.

⁶J. R. P. French and B. Raven, "The Bases of Social Power," in *Group Dynamics*, ed. D. Cartwright and A. Zander (New York: Harper & Row, 1959). Note that these five forms are essentially neutral, not necessarily incarnating any moral or ethical implications in their approach. Any of the forms can be used appropriately or inappropriately. In crisis or military situations, commanding may be the only option.

⁷N. Tehrani, in Bultena and Whatcott, "Bushwacked at Work," p. 654.

⁸Summarized from M. Stephens and V. Marsden, "Bullying of Senior Managers: An Ethnography," May 20, 2009, www.ecu.edu.au/lift/pdc/wil/98part4.rtf.

⁹R. Hull and L. J. Peter, *The Peter Principle: Why Things Always Go Wrong* (New York: Collins Business, 2009). See also A. Pluchino, C. Garofalo and A. Rapisarda, "The Peter Principle Revisited: A Computational Study," July 2, 2009, retrieved August 25, 2009, www.citebase.org/abstract?id=oai%3AarXiv.org%3A0907.0455.

¹⁰S. B. Sample, *The Contrarian's Guide to Leadership* (San Francisco: Jossey-Bass, 2002), pp. 7-20.

¹¹Leonardo DiCaprio, quoted in *The Oregonian*, November 7, 2004.

¹²This does not mean that the actions of leaders in designing and acting on imagery is necessarily bad. See, for example, Lee Bolman and Terrence Deal's discussion of the symbolic frame, which conveys the significance of ritual and ceremony to the culture of the organization (*Reframing Organizations*, 4th ed. [San Francisco: Wiley, 2011]) and Jean Lipman-Blumen's discussion of the Instrumental-Personal achieving style of the connective leader who manages symbolism and uses ritual and costume to communicate their message (*Connective Leadership* [New York: Oxford University Press, 2000). Both describe how certain associations are important for leadership to be effective.

¹³What Mihaly Csikszentmihalyi describes as memes (*The Evolving Self* [New York: HarperCollins, 1994])—these take our energy and attention.

¹⁴M. De Pree, *Leadership Is an Art* (New York: Doubleday, 1989), p. 11.

¹⁵Ibid.

¹⁶R. Greenleaf and L. Spears, *Servant Leadership* (New York: Paulist Press, 2002).

¹⁷Ibid., pp. 13-14.

¹⁸W. Bennis and D. A. Heenan, *Co-Leaders: The Power of Great Partnerships* (New York: Wiley, 1999); J. A. Conger and C. L. Pearce, *Shared Leadership: Reframing the Hows and Whys of Leadership* (Thousand Oaks, Calif.: Sage Publications, 2002); J. Lipman-Blumen, *Connective Leadership: Managing in a Changing World* (New York: Oxford University Press, 2000).

[19]M. De Pree, *Leading Without Power: Finding Hope in Serving Community* (San Francisco: Jossey-Bass, 2003).

[20]But even this idea is not always simple because good employees learn how to "manage" their bosses, according to Drucker and others. See Collins, *Good to Great and the Social Sectors*, p. 13.

[21]P. Drucker, *Managing the Non-Profit Organization* (New York: HarperBusiness, 1990), p. 343.

[22]Ibid., p. 27.

[23]J. T. Minor, "A Case of Complex Governance," *Journal of the Professoriate* 1, no. 2 (2006): 22-37.

[24]J. Lipman-Blumen, "Toxic Leadership: A Conceptual Framework," accessed July 7, 2012, www.achievingstyles.com/articles/toxic_leadership_a_conceptual _framework.pdf.

Chapter 3: These People Can't Be Led

[1]B. Kellerman, *Followership: How Followers Are Creating Change and Changing Leaders*, Center for Public Leadership (New York: Harvard Business School Press, 2008), p. 241, emphasis in the original.

[2]W. C. Wright, *Relational Leadership* (Downers Grove, Ill.: InterVarsity Press, 2012), p. 33; see also J. Rost, "Followership: An Outmoded Concept," in *The Art of Followership*, ed. R. E. Riggio, I. Chaleff and J. Lipman-Blumen (San Francisco: Jossey-Bass, 2008), p. 56.

[3]D. M. Scholer, "Phoebe/diakonos," *Corpus Paul Archives*, January 27, 2000, retrieved November 15, 2009, http://lists.ibiblio.org/pipermail /corpus-paul/20000128/001589.html.

[4]R. A. Heifetz and M. Linsky, "Anchor Yourself," in *Leadership on the Line: Staying Alive Through the Dangers of Leading* (Boston: Harvard Business School Press, 2002), p. 13.

[5]B. DePaulo, "Believing the Lies You Tell," retrieved November 11, 2010, http://roomfordebate.blogs.nytimes.com/2010/05/19/politicians-and-their -fake-war-stories/.

[6]I. Janis, "Groupthink: The Desperate Drive for Consensus at Any Cost," in *Classics of Organization Theory*, ed. J. Ott, J. Shafritz and K. S. Jang (Belmont, Calif.: Wadsworth, 2005), p. 185.

[7]Ibid., p. 187.

[8]N. J. Fast and L. Z. Tiedens, "Blame Contagion: The Automatic Transmission of Self-Serving Attributions," *Journal of Experimental Social Psychology* 46 (2010): 97-106.

[9]M. Pearson, "Workplace Shaman: Blaming Culture May Miss Real Culprit," *National Post/Canadian News, Financial News and Opinion*, September 1, 2009, retrieved November 29, 2010, www.nationalpost.com/life /travel/Workplace+Shaman+Blaming+culture+miss+real+culprit/1951613 /story.html.

[10]T. B. Savage, *Power Through Weakness: Paul's Understanding of the Christian Ministry in 2 Corinthians*, Society for New Testament Studies Monograph Series (Cambridge: Cambridge University Press, 2004).

[11]Ibid., p. 55.

[12]While the Western world continues to move toward more "flat" organizations, almost all organizations have some kind of hierarchy, whether explicit or tacit. Even informally, there are power structures.

[13]K. Ludeman and E. Erlandson, *Alpha Male Syndrome* (Boston: Harvard Business School Press, 2006), p. 51.

[14]Workplace Bullying and Trauma Institute, Bellingham, Wash., 2007 survey, p. 10, retrieved August 6, 2012, www.workplacebullying.org /docs/WBIsurvey2007.pdf.

[15]H. Leymann, "The Content and Development of Mobbing at Work," *European Journal of Work and Organizational Psychology* 5, no. 2 (1996): 165-84.

[16]K. Westhues, in C. Bultena and R. Whatcott, "Bushwacked at Work: A Comparative Analysis of Mobbing and Bullying at Work," *Proceedings of ASBBS* 15, no. 1 (2008): 652-66, emphasis added.

[17]K. Westhues, *Checklist of Mobbing Indicators*, 2006, retrieved November 28, 2010, http://arts.uwaterloo.ca/~kwesthue/checklist.htm.

[18]O. Brafman and R. A. Beckstrom, *The Starfish and the Spider: The Unstoppable Power of Leaderless Organizations* (New York: Portfolio, 2006).

[19]R. Tucker, "My Calvin Seminary Story," retrieved August 6, 2012, www .ruthtucker.net.

[20]J. Collins's theories about executive and legislative leadership, discussed in chapter one of this book, provide background for this idea.

[21]B. Kellerman, *Followership: How Followers Are Creating Change and Changing Leaders*, Center for Public Leadership (New York: Harvard Business School Press, 2008), p. 227.

[22]N. Davenport, G. P. Elliott and R. D. Schwartz, *Mobbing: Emotional Abuse in the American Workplace*, 3rd ed. (Ames, Iowa: Civil Society Publishing, 2005), p. 21.

Chapter 4: System Fatigue Syndrome

[1]D. McGregor, *The Human Side of Enterprise* (New York: McGraw-Hill Professional, 1960).

[2]J. Gall, *General Systemantics* (New York: New York Times Book Company, 1977). Quotes from appendix 1.

[3]L. K. Johnson, "Silo Busting from the Top," *Harvard Management Update* (2006). Reprint # U0607A, p. 1.

[4]P. M. Lencioni, *Silos, Politics and Turf Wars: A Leadership Fable About Destroying the Barriers That Turn Colleagues Into Competitors* (San Francisco: Jossey-Bass, 2006), p. 175.

[5]E. H. Baker, "Get Out of the Silo," January 20, 2009, retrieved September 25, 2009, www.strategy-business.com/article/li00108?gko=9641f.

[6]P. Drucker, "The American CEO," *Wall Street Journal*, December 30, 2004.

Chapter 5: Is "Christian Organization" an Oxymoron?

[1]M. Uarte, "Doctor, What's Happening to My Company?" Universia Knowledge@Wharton (n.d.), retrieved April 20, 2010, www.wharton.universia.net/index.cfm?fa=printArticle&ID=1562&language=English.

[2]D. Willard, *The Divine Conspiracy* (San Francisco: HarperOne, 1998), pp. 67-68.

[3]R. D. Winter and S. C. Hawthorne, "The Two Structures of God's Redemptive Mission," in *Perspectives on the World Christian Movement: A Reader* (Pasadena, Calif.: William Carey Library, 1981), pp. 220-30.

[4]In Christian theology, a *sodality* is a form of the church universal expressed in specialized, task-oriented form, as opposed to the church in its local, diocesan form (*modality*). In North America, the name *sodality* is most commonly used by groups in the Roman Catholic Church, where they are also referred to as *confraternities*. Sodalities among Protestants can be illustrated by mission organizations, societies and specialized ministries that have proliferated particularly since the advent of the modern missions movement. These are often called "parachurch" organizations.

[5]J. Hilgers, "Sodality," in *The Catholic Encyclopedia* (New York: Robert Appleton Company, 1912), retrieved November 7, 2009, www.newadvent.org/cathen/14120a.htm.

[6]J. Surowiecki, *The Wisdom of Crowds* (New York: Anchor, 2005).

[7]J. Gravois, "Mob Rule," *Chronicle of Higher Education*, April 14, 2006. Sunstein wrote *Infotopia: How Many Minds Produce Knowledge* (New York: Oxford University Press, 2006), building on Surowiecki.

[8]P. M. Senge, *The Fifth Discipline: The Art and Practice of the Learning Organization* (New York: Currency, 2006).

[9]E. H. Schein, *Organizational Culture and Leadership*, 3rd ed. (San Francisco: Jossey-Bass, 2004), p. 2.

[10]G. Hofstede and G. H. Hofstede, *Cultures and Organizations: Software for the Mind* (New York: McGraw-Hill, 2004), p. 282.

[11]Y. S. Jang, J. S. Ott and J. M. Shafritz, *Classics of Organization Theory (with InfoTrac)*, 6th ed. (Belmont, Calif.: Wadsworth Publishing, 2004), p. 361.

[12]Schein, *Organizational Culture and Leadership*, pp. 9-10.

[13]G. L. Neilson, B. A. Pasternack and K. E. Van Nuys, "The Passive-Aggressive Organization," *Harvard Business Review*, October 2005, Reprint #0510E, pp. 1-10.

[14]P. Drucker, *The Essential Drucker* (New York: Harper Business, 2007), p. 45.

[15]C. Edwards, "Intel: Supercharging Silicon Valley," *BusinessWeek* (n.d.), retrieved April 20, 2010, www.businessweek.com/magazine/content/04_40 /b3902032_mz072.htm.

[16]D. Willard, "The Fine Texture of Life in the Kingdom of the Heavens," Living in the Kingdom of God Conference, Folsom, California, Spring 2002.

[17]D. Gonzalez, "A Pastor's Job Offers Become a Curse," *New York Times*, April 22, 2010, retrieved August 6, 2012, www.nytimes.com/2010/04/23/nyregion/23hire .html?pagewanted=all.

[18]Even the *New York Times* approves. See N. D. Kristof, "Learning From the Sin of Sodom," *New York Times* (n.d.), retrieved April 26, 2010, www.ny times.com/2010/02/28/opinion/28kristof.html?scp=1&sq=%22World%20 Vision%22&st=cse.

[19]M. Weber, *Economy and Society: An Outline of Interpretive Sociology* (Berkeley: University of California Press, 1978), p. 213.

[20]J. Burns, *Leadership* (New York: Harper & Row, 1978), pp. 19-20. Emphasis in the original.

Chapter 6: The Management of Sin

[1]Jim Collins sees a "culture of niceness" as a barrier to effectiveness. J. Collins, *Good to Great and the Social Sectors* (New York: HarperCollins, 2005), p. 32.

[2]H. Gardner, *Responsibility at Work: How Leading Professionals Act (or Don't Act) Responsibly* (San Francisco: Jossey-Bass, 2007), p. 22.

[3]R. A. Emmons, *The Psychology of Ultimate Concern: Motivation and Spirituality in Personality* (New York: Guilford Press, 1999), quoted in ibid., p. 23.

[4]Gardner, *Responsibility at Work*, p. 23.

[5]A. Redpath, *Blessings Out of Buffetings* (Grand Rapids: Revell, 1984).

[6]N. T. Wright, *Evil & the Justice of God* (Downers Grove, Ill.: InterVarsity Press, 2006), p. 161.

[7]B. L. Ramm, *The Right, the Good & the Happy* (Waco, Tex.: Word, 1971), p. 46.

[8]Addressed in detail in a variety of books by Richard Foster; also in D. Willard, *The Spirit of the Disciplines: Understanding How God Changes Lives* (New York: HarperCollins, 1990).

[9]See C. Argyris and D. Schön, *Organizational Learning: A Theory of Action Perspective* (Reading, Mass: Addison Wesley, 1978); Peter Senge, *The Fifth Discipline* (New York: Crown Business, 2006).

[10]Quoted in A. Pattakos, *Prisoners of Our Thoughts* (San Francisco: Berrett-Koehler, 2004), p. 124.

[11]Ramm, *The Right, the Good & the Happy*, p. 42.

[12]For one of the most cogent discussions of these issues see A. Hirschman, *Exit, Voice and Loyalty* (Boston: Harvard University Press, 1970).

[13]"In the early years of [the twentieth century], the most highly respected diplomat of all the great powers was the German ambassador in London. He was clearly destined for great things—to become his country's foreign minister, at least, if not its federal chancellor. Yet in 1906 he abruptly resigned rather than preside over a dinner given by the diplomatic corps for Edward VII. The king was a notorious womanizer and made it clear what kind of dinner he wanted. The ambassador is reported to have said, 'I refuse to see a pimp in the mirror in the morning when I shave.' This is the mirror test. . . . To work in an organization whose value system is unacceptable or incompatible with one's own condemns a person both to frustration and to nonperformance." P. Drucker, *Management Challenges for the 21st Century* (New York: Harper Business, 1999), p. 175.

[14]J. Wallis, "The Power of Reconciliation," *Sojourners Magazine*, April 6, 2011.

[15]K. Fong, "A Disturbing Question and a Determined Conviction on the Treatment of Women," http://blog.sojo.net/2010/03/08/a-disturbing -question-and-a-determined-conviction-on-the-treatment-of-women.

Chapter 7: Peter Drucker's "Meaningful Outside"

[1]A. G. Lafley, "What Only the CEO Can Do," *Harvard Business Review*, May 2009, http://hbr.harvardbusiness.org/2009/05/what-only-the-ceo-can-do/ib.

[2]P. Drucker, *Management Challenges for the 21st Century* (New York: Harper Business, 2001), p. 38.

[3]P. Drucker, *Management: Tasks, Responsibilities, Practices* (New York: Butterworth-Heinemann, 2004), p. 522.

[4]J. Collins, *Good to Great and the Social Sectors* (New York: HarperCollins, 2005), p. 17.

[5]R. Heifetz, *Leadership Without Easy Answers* (Boston: Harvard University Press, 1998), p. 14.

[6]Len Schlesinger, interviewed by Bill Hybels, Leadership Summit, Willow Creek Church, Barrington, Illinois, 1998.

[7]Drucker, *Management: Tasks, Responsibilities, Practices*, p. 121.

Chapter 8: Relationship Responsibility

[1]D. Goleman et al., *Primal Leadership* (Cambridge, Mass.: Harvard Business School Press, 2009), p. 104.

[2]P. Drucker, *Management: Tasks, Responsibilities, Practices*, (Woburn, Mass.: Butterworth-Heineman, 1999), p. 499.

[3]M. De Pree, *Leadership Is an Art* (New York: Crown Business, 2004), pp. 50-51.

[4]See J. Lipmen-Blumen, *The Allure of Toxic Leaders* (New York: Oxford University Press, 2006), chap. 13, pp. 235-56.

[5]J. Collins, *Good to Great and the Social Sectors* (New York: HarperCollins, 2005), p. 32.

[6]R. Heifetz and D. Laurie, "The Work of Leadership," *Harvard Business Review*, January-February 1997, pp. 124-34.

[7]D. A. Carson, *A Model of Christian Maturity: An Exposition of 2 Corinthians 10-13* (Grand Rapids: Baker, 2007), pp. 188-89.

[8]De Pree, *Leadership Is an Art*, p. 49.

[9]M. A. Hogg, "Social Identity Theory of Leadership," in *Leadership at the Crossroads*, vol. 1, *Leadership and Psychology*, ed. C. L. Hoyt, G. R. Goethals and D. R. Forsyth (Westport, Conn.: Praeger, 2008), p. 65.

[10]Ibid., p. 69.

[11]M. Hogg, *Academy of Management Review* 25, no. 1 (2000): 129.

[12]E. H. Schein, *Organizational Culture and Leadership* (New York: Wiley & Sons, 2010), p. 371.

[13]"Robert Lane, '74, Describes Deere Turnaround on 'CEO Exchange,'" University of Chicago, www.chicagobooth.edu/news/2007-03-27_CEO-exchange.aspx. In 2008, Deere was among the twenty-five most socially responsible companies in the United States.

[14]E. Schein, *Organizational Culture and Leadership*, 4th ed. (San Francisco: Jossey-Bass, 2010), p. 301.

[15]See M. Csikszentmihalyi, *Good Business* (New York: Penguin, 2004);

D. Goleman, R. Boyatzis, A. McKee, *Primal Leadership: Realizing the Power of Emotional Intelligence* (Boston: Harvard Business School Press, 2002).

[16]C. Dweck, in M. Krakovsky, "The Effort Effect," *Stanford Magazine*, retrieved August 6, 2012, www.stanfordalumni.org/news/magazine/2007/marapr/features/dweck.html.

[17]Drucker, *Management: Tasks, Responsibilities, Practices,* p. 457.

[18]Carson, *Model of Christian Maturity,* p. 160.

Chapter 9: Hope, Generosity and Power

[1]M. Wheatley, "Turning to One Another: Simple Conversations to Restore Hope to the Future," *Journal for Quality & Participation* 25, no. 2 (2002): 8-19, para. 31.

[2]One of our favorite lines to remind us of this is "Denial is not a river in Egypt!"

[3]M. De Pree, *Leadership Is an Art* (New York: Crown, 2004), p. 100.

[4]R. Heifetz, interviewed by W. C. Taylor, "The Leader of the Future," *Fast Company*, December 19, 2007, www.fastcompany.com/magazine/25/heifetz.html.

[5]Ibid.

[6]Ibid.

[7]Ibid.

[8]D. Hock, "The Art of Chaordic Leadership," *Leader To Leader Journal* (Winter 2000), http://www.hesselbeininstitute.org/knowledgecenter/journal.aspx?ArticleID=62.

[9]R. Heifetz, "Leader of the Future."

[10]A. O. Hirschman, *Exit, Voice, and Loyalty: Responses to Decline in Firms, Organizations, and States* (Cambridge, Mass.: Harvard University Press, 1970).

[11]Ibid., p. 80.

[12]Ibid.

[13]J. Welch, "The Best Managers Aren't Perfect but They Keep Getting Back on the Horse," retrieved August 15, 2009, www.managementhelp.info/Jack-Welch-Success-Getting-Back-Up-on-Horse/624.

[14]M. De Pree, *Leading Without Power* (San Francisco: Jossey-Bass, 2003), p. 151.

[15]J. Collins, *Good to Great* (New York: HarperCollins, 2005), p. 85.

[16]M. Csikszentmihalyi, *Good Business* (New York: Viking Adult, 2003), p. 165.

Chapter 10: Letting God

[1]G. E. Ladd, *The Presence of the Future: The Eschatology of Biblical Realism* (Grand Rapids: Eerdmans, 1974).